READING AND WRITING
IN HIGH SCHOOLS

The Authors

Eric Hobson is a doctoral candidate and graduate teaching associate in the Department of English at the University of Tennessee, Knoxville.

R. Baird Shuman is Professor of English and Director of English Education at the University of Illinois at Urbana-Champaign. Dr. Shuman is the author of *The First R: Fundamentals of Initial Reading Instruction* and of *Classroom Encounters: Problems, Case Studies, Solutions;* and the author or editor of these previous NEA publications: *The Beginning Teacher: A Practical Guide to Problem Solving* (with Robert J. Krajewski), *Education in the 80's: English*, and *Strategies in Teaching Reading: Secondary*.

The Advisory Panel

Frances R. Baron, Kindergarten Teacher, West Ottawa Public Schools, Holland, Michigan

June Russell Gilstad, Educational Consultant, Instructional Services, Kokomo, Indiana

Barbara A. Johnson, Humanities and English Teacher, Russellville High School, Arkansas

Mary Kramer, Professor, English Department, University of Lowell, Massachusetts

Marilyn Louwerens, Reading Teacher, Niceville High School, Florida

William McFarland, Principal, Prattville High School, Alabama

Margaret L. Petrella, Social Studies Teacher, South Carroll High School, Sykesville, Maryland

Phillip G. Wilson, English Teacher, Shawnee Mission West High School, Overland Park, Kansas

READING AND WRITING IN HIGH SCHOOLS:
A Whole-Language Approach

Eric Hobson
R. Baird Shuman

nea **PROFESSIONAL LIBRARY**
National Education Association
Washington, D.C.

Note

The opinions expressed in this publication should not be construed as representing the policy or position of the National Education Association. Materials published by the NEA Professional Library are intended to be discussion documents for educators who are concerned with specialized interests of the profession.

Library of Congress Cataloging-in-Publication Data

Hobson, Eric.
    Reading and writing in high schools : a whole-language approach /
Eric Hobson, R. Baird Shuman.
        p.   cm.—(Analysis and action series)
    Includes bibliographical references.
    ISBN 0-8106-3073-7
    1. Language experience approach in education—United States.
2. English language—Composition and exercises—Study and teaching
(Secondary)—United States.   3. Reading (Secondary).   I. Shuman, R.
Baird (Robert Baird), 1929–   II. Title.   III. Series.
LB1631.H553   1990
428.4'0712—dc20   89-49154
                                                                                    CPI

CONTENTS

INTRODUCTION

When we began to talk about writing this book, we thought we would focus on reading and writing in high schools in light of the whole-language movement that has recently changed a great deal of thinking about how people learn. As our research deepened, we began quickly to realize that to focus on individual communicative arts at the high school level runs counter to the whole-language philosophy. The academic environment that whole-language theory encourages, and that many high schools strive for, is one in which strict compartmentalization and departmentalization of information is unrealistic. Students are encouraged frequently to listen, to speak, to read, and to write in all areas of the curriculum and to begin asking the questions that reveal the dependence that exists between various bodies of knowledge. It soon became clear to us that all of the arts of communication overlap, interact, and impinge on each other. Major elements of our book necessarily do the same.

With the realization of these interrelationships came the decision to alter somewhat our original focus and to concentrate on the skills of decoding—reading and listening—and the skills of encoding—writing and speaking. We have not presented information about some of the other communicative skills, notably body language—facial expressions, gestures—although we acknowledge its importance and realize how significant a role it plays in the overall process of communicating. Anyone who has ever watched a group of students discuss the homecoming dance or the action of a recent football game, or who has listened to a clutch of teachers swap tales about students' antics knows that the body often tells us as much as the words being spoken.

We have attempted to suggest to teachers things they can do quite easily, and without special equipment, to enliven their students' approaches to learning those two skills that society demands of most people: reading and writing. Because we have found it impossible to divorce these skills from the related skills of listening and speaking, much of our book involves suggestions that engage two or more of these skills simultaneously. This is the way most of us use the skills of communication in our lives. Whether at home or at work, most of our activities require us to use our communicative skills to create bridges of meaning and intention, to create interrelationships.

Our conviction is that the best learning takes place when it is as closely related to the actual world of work as possible. Such learning fits into the vocational agenda of American education and taps into the utilitarian desires that motivate many students. We have attempted to provide teachers with a theoretical basis for the whole-language approach, but our major emphasis is on providing them with ways to implement this theoretical base that has been well documented in many of the books cited in our endnotes and in our annotated bibliography.

The exercises we suggest may not be appropriate to each reader's immediate teaching situation. We have, however, sought to generalize them in ways that will make possible adaptations that individual teachers in specific situations can employ as they tailor the exercises to their own classrooms and students.

One of the side benefits of the whole-language approach to teaching English is that it not only helps students to learn such specifics as grammar, usage, and mechanics in real and natural ways, but that it also provides teachers with opportunities to make linkages with the community, and to involve parents and other citizens in school activities. The public relations benefits of such interaction can be substantial, but they are dwarfed by the learning benefits that accrue to students through such an approach.

We wish you well as you work to bring about in your own teaching situation some of the changes we suggest. We know that you will be responsible as you work to achieve these changes. We hope also that you will be daring and willing to take occasional risks in order to bring about the sorts of change that only imaginative teachers can implement. We must also count on you to share with your colleagues and administrators some of the ideas you derive from this book.

—Eric Hobson
R. Baird Shuman

Chapter 1

HOW PEOPLE LEARN

Any discussion of teaching must inevitably evolve from questions about the nature of learners and the ways diverse groups of them happen to know what they know. The greatest learning spurt comes to everyone in the years between birth and age four. These are the egocentric years, the years when small children have to focus on themselves if they are to survive. Learning is an act of desperation for them. They work harder and more continuously at it in their earliest years than they ever will again—so continuously that adults sometimes grow impatient with their constant repetitions, their incessant questions.

These are the wonder years, the years in which a somewhat neutral organism takes on the colorations of a family, of a community, of a whole culture. These are concept-building years. Small children are blotters soaking up everything that surrounds them, internalizing quickly the mores of their families as well as the structure of the language or languages spoken around them. By the time they are six months old they understand much of what they hear. By the time they are a year old they begin to speak. By the time they are 30 months old they can use all the grammatical structures their language environment offers, even though they are not consciously aware that they are using simple, compound, complex, and compound-complex sentences. They punctuate words in series and ends of constructions by pausing when they need to. They move from one tense to another with relative ease. At this stage, it is interesting to observe the things children say, often things that cause adults to correct them. If they say, "Daddy drived away," doting adults will usually respond, "Daddy *drove* away." Literate adults insist on the irregular form, acknowledging that *to drive* is a strong verb, whereas children, who are internalizing the grammatical structure of tenses, initially regularize many strong verbs, demonstrating that they are forming important generalizations about the way their language operates. They are using language intuitively, adopting the method that children through the ages have used as they gained mastery of their native tongues. Children at this stage intuitively implement language in the most economical way, often reflecting linguistic change that is occurring generally in the language even as they struggle to master it.

9

HOW CHILDREN GROW
FROM BELIEVERS TO SKEPTICS

Young children are fast learners. They pluck information from every source they encounter, from the disparate noise that surrounds them, from what they see and feel and taste and touch. They are tiny bastions of sensation and of sense-making, learning from experiences they have in their surroundings during every waking moment.

As children grow older, they continue to learn, but much of their learning occurs within more formal structures than they were exposed to in the home. Modern children encounter increasingly formal structures ever earlier because more of them are sent to nursery- and pre-schools while their parents work. Such schools impose on them interaction with substantial numbers of other children—strangers to them at first—that children in earlier societies did not experience in the same structured way. The latter did not go to school until they were five or six years old. The interaction young children a generation or two ago had at home with their siblings was different from that experienced by their counterparts today in their dealings with peers in their early school encounters. Fifty years ago, familial interaction was often controlled by one or both parents as well as by older siblings. Now it is controlled for many of a child's waking hours by someone outside the family who is dealing with several children at once.

Some years ago, Charles Keller, sponsored by a major foundation, did a longitudinal study of the development of students in school settings. As he neared the end of this 12-year study in which he had followed children from ages 6 to 18, one of the authors met him and asked, "What is the most striking thing you have learned from your observations?" After pondering the question, he responded thoughtfully, "What strikes me most is a puzzlement with which I am left. As these youngsters matured into adolescence, I was left with a nagging question: 'I wonder where the wonder went?'"

Keller touched on a question that puzzles many high school teachers, especially those who have worked with students in the lower grades or who have frequent opportunities to associate with younger children. Until a certain age, most young people are full of wonder. They quest relentlessly for experience and information. They are egocentric enough to insist on developing and asserting their own personalities.

But all at once something happens that began much earlier when they reached the age at which socialization set in, at which egocentricity was downplayed, usually at about the time they began the primary grades. As they develop, belonging, which the younger child takes for granted, counts more to them than anything else in the world.

10

Children move from this stage into the period—roughly coinciding with the onset of puberty—when being cool is valued to the point that achieving the dispassionate aura of coolness becomes in many young people tantamount to a refusal to learn—a refusal to learn, at least, the things teachers and parents want them to learn.

Learning theorists have generally recognized this period of development and have labeled it in various ways. Piaget says that "the adolescent's adoption of adult roles certainly presupposes those affective and intellectual tools whose spontaneous development is exactly what distinguishes adolescence from childhood."[1]* He goes on to characterize adolescents as differing from children because of their tendency to think beyond the present, to be more future oriented than children are.

Perhaps it is best to describe this stage of development in most American youth as a period of youthful skepticism. This is the time at which most young people regularly begin to question authority figures, to startle them with outlandish dress and wild hairdos—that they desperately want their elders to notice and react to—and to work on developing their own personalities. In many adolescents, these new personalities seem totally contradictory to those of the people who have brought them up—parents, guardians, siblings, teachers, and others who have been their earliest models.

THE WINNOWING PROCESS

For good or bad, change in the twentieth century has been dizzying—more so, perhaps, than in any preceding hundred years because this century has made human communication over enormous distances a reality. In prehistory, Phoenician traders and other intrepid adventurers conquered the oceans. Their vision, heroism, and curiosity set humankind on its way and by a circuitous route led to the accomplishments of the twentieth century in the fields of transportation and communication.

We have conquered space! Humans can talk with each other across great oceans. Humans can be whisked from Washington to Paris, New York to London on supersonic commercial airliners in just over three hours. Humans have set foot on the moon. Space probes have landed on Mars. Earthly vehicles are at this moment reaching the outer limits of our universe and sending their messages back over more than three billion miles, revising drastically our understanding of the universe. Radio, television, telephones, computers, electronic mail, and fax machines have

---

*Superior numbers appearing in the text refer to the Notes at the end of the chapter.

supplanted communication by tom-toms and smoke signals and, even to an extent, the postal service.

The implications of this conquest are enormous. We still do not understand them fully because we cling to past values, many of which are irrelevant to contemporary society. An example of human atavism is seen in widespread and much-publicized complaints from the public that American school children cannot read and write. Many of the critics protest that high schools graduate students who have not mastered the basic competencies one expects of high school graduates. *Illiteracy* and *innumeracy* are terms frequently encountered in the lexicon of such heated discussions and debate.

School districts and state educational systems have responded to such criticisms by instituting minimal competency examinations at various stages of students' educations, by demanding that teacher training be improved, and by lengthening the school day and the school year. These efforts are usually well intended, but they often are unsuccessful and unrealistic. Our national strength depends upon our having as well educated and effectively performing a populace as we can, but the rush to testing and measuring has not assured the nation convincingly that schools, through increased formal evaluation, can produce better students.

HIGH SCHOOL GRADUATES OF 1900

We must not lose sight of one crucial truth, which may at first seem to contradict what we have just written. In the United States in the year 1900, *HIGH SCHOOL GRADUATES WERE LITERATE.* "Aha," you say, "so the schools *are* declining!" Not so. Although this accurate claim about the abilities of earlier high school graduates sounds wonderful and seems to confirm that American education has declined to the point of jeopardizing our national future as significantly as the *Nation at Risk* report suggests, the information left out is that in the year 1900, about 10 percent of the population aged 17 to 19 completed high school. This 10 percent was exposed to a college preparatory curriculum—the only secondary school curriculum available—and all high school graduates expected to attend college or would, as in many cases they did, end their formal educations and become teachers.

What about the other 90 percent? Because American society was still essentially agrarian and because most people lived in small towns or on farms, this 90 percent was able to become contributing members of a society structured in a relatively simple way. More hands were always needed on farms, and for many families it was an economic sacrifice to allow their children to stay in school even to the eighth grade. In most cases,

12

seventh or eighth grade corresponded roughly with the onset of puberty, and the physical activity of farming helped to control the rampaging hormones of teenagers until they were 15 or 16, ages at which they were considered marriageable.

As industry outpaced farming as the largest employer in the early twentieth century, the entire demographic situation in this country changed substantially. The mechanization of farming reduced the need for the huge numbers of farm personnel required only a decade or two before. The American population began to be centered in cities and towns rather than in the country or in tiny villages.

THE RISE OF INDUSTRIAL SOCIETY

Industrialized society demanded more specialized skills than farming. As a result, the whole educational establishment expanded to meet the needs of the nation's rapidly growing industries, first by inventing the junior high school, originally designed to encourage students to finish ninth grade rather than leaving school at the end of eighth. With the passage of the Smith-Hughes National Vocational Education Act of 1917, national attention was focused on offering vocational education at the secondary level throughout the nation, thereby opening the senior high school to many young people who a decade earlier would not have continued their educations.

Simultaneously, more stringent school attendance laws were enacted and enforced, spurred largely by industry's attempt to keep young, unskilled workers out of the labor market. Many jobs that required no extraordinary skills were open only to high school graduates. Companies that adopted such hiring standards were essentially allowing the schools to make the first cut in their pool of job applicants, thereby reducing the pool to a manageable size.

THE RUSH TO EVALUATION

From all this social change has grown a situation in which the public and many governmental agencies condemn modern education, call it a failure, demand tougher standards, and call for extensive, sequential testing to assure the enforcement of these standards. For many students, going to school means being tested continually. When modern high school students are not actually taking tests, they are often being prepared specifically to take tests that loom in their futures, being schooled not only in substantive material but also being taught "test-savviness," the achievement of which is tantamount to succeeding educationally in most academic venues today.

Rote memory was emphasized in many early school systems from the eighteenth century on because the schools that grew out of the Industrial Revolution in Britain were charged with teaching students two fundamental behaviors: punctuality and obedience. Although such education rewarded the dutiful and compliant, it has not been found to be a notably effective way of preparing people to function productively in the world as it has moved to more participatory societies, which require a clear-thinking, literate electorate.

It may still be desirable for some people to master activities that require rote learning, such as the multiplication tables, but our society has moved quickly from needing people who have memorized to needing people who can reason and solve complex problems. United States society has moved from being essentially a producer economy to being a service economy with incredibly sophisticated technologies available to its members.

As this change occurred, it made knowing even the multiplication tables less necessary—if not less desirable—than was once the case. The common, inexpensive pocket calculators sold at any drugstore hold more mathematical information than most human minds ever commanded. The lap-top computer, soon to be replaced by the *hand-held* computer, has put encyclopedic knowledge at every user's fingertips even in the most remote areas.

In light of these changes, and in light of the broadening of the high school to include 97 percent of the population rather than the previous 10 percent, misunderstandings have occurred. Members of the public, usually resistant to change, cherish their notion of what high school graduates were at the turn of the century. Lacking a total historical view of the past, they point accusing fingers at today's schools and teachers because today's high school students do not conform universally to their distorted and outmoded images of what constitutes high school graduates.

THE VOCATIONAL NATURE
OF ALL EFFECTIVE EDUCATION

All education has initially been designed to fulfill vocational ends. When Harvard College opened in 1636 with a handful of students and a few minimally trained faculty, it offered a limited curriculum: Latin, Greek, Hebrew, philosophy, and theology. Its aim was to provide clergymen for the raw new society that was developing on our shores. The limited curriculum was directly vocational and met the specific needs of the first students who attended Harvard. Men—in those days women did not receive a higher education—who wished to study for other vocations like medicine or law usually went to Germany or France or Britain.

Oddly enough, many later schools that grew up in Harvard's shadow continued to retain some of its requirements, particularly training in Latin and Greek, even though these new schools were training students for fields vastly different from theology in which a knowledge of the languages of the Old (Hebrew) and New (Greek) Testaments and of the language of the early church fathers (Latin) was indisputably helpful. Until the mid 1850s, everyone who received a bachelor's degree in the United States, regardless of field, had a foundation in classical languages. Some educators justified this emphasis by saying that studying classical languages trained the mind, although later psychologists convincingly disproved the so-called faculty theory of learning that such thinking reflects.

Education becomes indefensible only when those who provide it lose sight of the vocational aims it seeks to serve. If the reason for demanding Latin and Greek of all college graduates until the mid-nineteenth century was that it had always been a requirement for a bachelor's degree, then the argument was reductive and the requirement absurd—as many educational reformers in the later nineteenth century finally got the public to realize.

WHO ARE TODAY'S HIGH SCHOOL STUDENTS?

Today's high school students are as diverse as the total populations of the communities from which they come. As long as we compel school attendance to age 16 or 17, this situation will persist. In public education, there is no educationally elite group; everyone who is compelled by law to attend school must be served.

It is for the public benefit that as many as possible of those students who attend school be retained to graduation, whatever their abilities and disabilities. They can learn in secondary schools skills that will benefit them throughout their lives. Mastery of these skills will make them more productive citizens if the curriculum permits such schools to accommodate the needs of their diverse student bodies.

From a practical standpoint, high school graduates—regardless of what they have studied or of how well they have done in their studies—benefit society because

1. during their lifetimes they pay substantially more in taxes than nongraduates;

15

2. fewer of them end up in prison than do high school dropouts;
3. fewer of them end up in mental institutions than do high school dropouts; and
4. they generally live more fulfilling lives than their counterparts who have not completed high school.

THE RENEWED EMPHASIS
ON TESTING AND MEASUREMENT

The renewed emphasis on testing and measurement during the decade of the 1980s suggests to many people who have thought through the situation a mindset that presumes society can be improved by establishing an intellectually elite class. Those who favor testing and measurement deny any such motives, protesting that they merely want to be assured that students with high school diplomas can perform at certain minimal levels. This is not the place to enter that explosive debate. It is necessary, however, to mention that the minimal-competency folk have applied pressure to make schools more test-centered than they were 10 years ago. A reaction to the increasing emphasis on testing began before the mid-1980s, when some reputable educators began to question the validity of putting as much emphasis on testing as schools recently have done.[2] This dispute will not be settled soon. Certainly college-bound students will continue to be subjected to the batteries of tests we are all familiar with and probably to forms of tests we have not yet dreamed of.

On behalf of such test-making organizations as the American College Testing Service (ACTS) and the Educational Testing Service (ETS), one must acknowledge that efforts are being made to test students in ways that demand reasoning and problem solving and that go far beyond the sort of questioning that encourages mostly rote learning. Schools, especially at the secondary level, would be remiss if they did not prepare their students for the tests they will all necessarily face in their futures.

To make schools lockstep institutions designed to train people in test-taking, however, is to cast upon them an Orwellian shadow that will discourage many marginal students from finishing school and that will not achieve the most desirable results with those who conform and allow themselves to be subjected to such a curriculum. A vast world exists beyond evaluation, as important as evaluation is. Many of the world's most dynamic leaders in every field have not tested well and have been either marginal students or dropouts. They, along with their test-savvy counterparts, contribute to society's good. Schools need to offer their examphobic students opportunities to perform in the ways they perform best.

16

What is necessary now in senior high school is a balance between the realities that face students in the world and the implementation of pedagogical techniques based on the best information learning theorists have provided through reliable and exhaustive research. Such research indicates that the whole-language approach more than any other currently available to educators helps students achieve a continuing aptitude for dealing with language in all its four aspects: speaking, listening, writing, and reading.

Notes

1. In Howard E. Gruber and J. Jacques Voneche, eds., *The Essential Piaget: An Interpretive Reference and Guide* (New York: Basic Books, 1977), p. 436. This quotation is originally found in Piaget's collaboration with Barbel Inhelder, *The Growth of Logical Thinking* (1955).
2. See especially Carol Gilles, Mary Bixby, Paul Crowley, Shirley R. Crenshaw, Margaret Henrichs, Frances E. Reynolds, and Donelle Pyle, eds., *Whole Language Strategies for Secondary School Students* (New York: Richard C. Owen Publishers, 1988); Kenneth Goodman, E. Brooks Smith, Robert Meredith, and Yetta Goodman, *Language and Thinking in School—A Whole Language Curriculum*, 3d ed. (New York: Richard C. Owen Publishers, 1987); Lucy Calkins, *The Art of Teaching Writing* (Portsmouth, N.H.: Heinemann, 1986); Kenneth Goodman, Yetta Goodman, and Wendy Hood, eds., *The Whole Language Evaluation Book* (Portsmouth, N.H.: Heinemann, 1989); Gary Manning and Maryann Manning, eds., *Whole Language: Beliefs and Practices, K–8* (Washington, D.C.: National Education Association, 1989); Gary Manning, Maryann Manning, and Roberta Long, *Reading and Writing in the Middle Grades: A Whole-Language View* (Washington, D.C.: National Education Association, 1990); and Judith M. Newman, ed., *Whole Language—Theory in Use* (Portsmouth, N.H.: Heinemann, 1985).

Chapter 2

WHAT IS THE WHOLE-LANGUAGE APPROACH?

The whole-language approach to learning the skills of human communication focuses centrally upon the learner. Teachers committed to this approach do a great deal of what Yetta Goodman calls "kidwatching." They stand back as teachers and make a concerted effort to learn as much as they can about the students they are going to work with—their interests, their worries, their enthusiasms, their problems, their loyalties, their commitments, their aspirations, their beliefs, their skills, their talents, their loves, their hatreds, their successes, their failures, their understandings, their misunderstandings, their disappointments, their dreams, and their purposes in life.

HOW DOES THE WHOLE-LANGUAGE APPROACH WORK IN THE CLASSROOM?

On the classroom level, this process of discovery in itself involves the whole of language. Students talk about themselves, and others listen to them talk; students write about themselves, and others read what they have written. These early writing ventures are among the most important activities students engage in during a whole year in an English class. They begin to suggest the focus of the class. They help to establish the climate of trust and mutual respect that lubricates the gears of effective learning activities; they encourage all the students to look into themselves and write about what they discover within.

The Socratic imperative, "Know thyself," underlies learning activities of this sort early in the year and will pervade them as other activities are built upon them throughout the year. As the year progresses, most teachers will involve students in work that moves into ever-broader spheres, progressing from writing or talking about oneself to writing or talking about oneself interacting with other people. From that point, teachers can gradually encourage students to focus on issues further outside their own spheres: school, community, state, national, international, global, and cosmic concerns, all of which are also personal concerns for everyone who is affected by them in some way.

BEGINNING THE SCHOOL YEAR

The writing at this stage should be informal, *expressive*, as James Britton calls it. It need not be in the form of a finished essay, which Britton calls *transactional* writing.[1] A teacher who thinks it is appropriate to have some students read Robert Cormier's *The Chocolate War*[2] might lead toward this reading early in the term by asking students to work with the following questions—which most of them will not regard as a writing assignment but will embrace as an assignment that helps them learn something about themselves and about their classmates.

Exercise 2.1

1. Have you ever been in a situation where you thought you had to do something you really opposed doing? Tell about it. What did you end up doing?
2. Did you ever do anything you really didn't think it was right for you to do? If so, why did you do it? How did it make you feel to do it?
3. Have you ever stood up for your principles even though you knew you would be punished or penalized for doing so? If so, tell about it.
4. Do you know anyone who has gotten into trouble for sticking to his or her principles? Tell about that person. Do you admire people like this or do you think they are foolish?
5. What figures in history come to mind as people who have had to pay a significant penalty for adhering to their principles? Tell about one or more of them.

These activities help students to
1. analyze their own beliefs,
2. assess their ability to defend their beliefs,
3. formulate logical arguments,
4. evaluate their beliefs in a historical context.

Exercise 2.2

When you finish working on this exercise, think through the following problem:

A physician divorced her husband four years ago. The court gave her custody of their teenage daughter, allowing the father, also a physician, the right to keep the daughter with him on alternate weekends. The mother soon suspected that the father was abusing the girl when she stayed with him. Her daughter finally tearfully confirmed her mother's suspicions. The mother sought to have the court order changed, but did not have enough solid evidence to persuade the judge that the daughter was in peril and that the father should not have access to her. The father denied the charges. The mother did not want her daughter, who was already terribly upset, to be forced to testify in court and to be subjected to the trauma of cross-examination. She resolved the situation by refusing to permit her daughter to spend alternate weekends with her father to prevent her having to spend time with a man of whom she had become terrified.

The father now sued for full custody, citing the mother's violation of the original court order as the basis for his petition. The court granted his petition. The court ordered the mother to turn the girl over to the father.

When she refused to do so and refused to reveal where the daughter, whom she had now sent away, was hiding, the mother was sentenced to jail for contempt of court, her term to run for as long as she defied the court order. She is now entering her third year in jail, and she intends to remain there, obviously at enormous personal sacrifice, for as long as she has to in order to protect her daughter's interests. She recently said she is more comfortable in jail knowing her daughter is safe than she would be at home fearing that her daughter was being exploited.

You may want to use this news story or recent news stories similar to it. The daily newspaper provides teachers with much raw material. The more current the material teachers use, the higher will be the interest level. Exercises like these entice students into thinking, writing, talking, and listening to what other students say. They use all their communication skills to deal with situations from real life and are also encouraged (Exercise 2.1, Item 5) to think historically about the basic question. Exercise 2.1 is designed specifically to move students from taking an introspective look at themselves to taking a look at people within their own spheres, and finally to looking back in history to people who have faced comparable dilemmas.

By proceeding in this order, some of the students will begin to see the universality of the dilemmas people face and will realize that such dilemmas have faced humankind throughout the ages. Possibly they will recently have seen a movie (like *Casualties of War*) or a television drama (like *Tailspin*) that poses exactly the type of questions posed here. Thinking through Exercise 2.2 serves two purposes:

1. It gives students who work quickly something to ponder while other students are finishing their work; and
2. it brings a real-life problem into the classroom, helping students to appreciate that their English class is neither remote from the real world nor oblivious to its problems.

In exercises like these, the four basic communicative skills are interwoven and are used interactively; students *read* the questions, the problem posed, and possibly each other's papers; they *write* their responses; they *talk* about their responses; and they *listen* to their classmates as they respond in class to the various questions and to the problem, probably engaging in dialogue with them. This exercise in itself suggests all sorts of other exercises. Teachers can use some of the following productively.

Exercise 2.3

1. Write a letter to the judge who sentenced the physician in the case given above. Either comment or object to the judge's action.
2. Write a letter to your state senator about the jailing of the physician.
3. Write a letter from a historical figure to someone in your class explaining why you (assuming the role of the historical figure) stood up for your principles.
4. Pose as the mate of someone who has been jailed for sticking to his or her principles. You are at home alone with your three children. Your income has been drastically reduced. If your mate gives in, he or she will be released at once.
5. Write a balanced article for the school newspaper in which you discuss the physician's imprisonment both from her standpoint and from the standpoint of the judge who sentenced her.
6. With several classmates, engage in an improvisation based on one of the situations in items 1 through 5 above.
7. With several classmates, act out the courtroom scene in which the physician is sentenced to jail for contempt of court.
8. Assuming that the physician in question earned an average

21

yearly income of $133,506 over the past five years and that she pays a combined state and federal income tax of 42 percent (35 percent federal, 7 percent state) on her earnings plus a 6 percent state sales tax on average purchases of $29,297 a year, write a letter to the editor of the local newspaper in the city in which she lived and practiced medicine that tells how much a month the state and the federal government are losing in taxes by her incarceration. Note also the loss to the community.

9. Hold interviews with five classmates in which you get their opinions about this physician's case. Then, write an "As They See It" public opinion column for the school newspaper.
10. On a cassette, tape a radio editorial about the case of someone who has been penalized for standing up for his or her principles. Interview people for this assignment if you like.

These activities help students to
1. organize arguments,
2. evaluate conflicting points of view,
3. realize some practical outcomes of taking unpopular ideological stands,
4. use a variety of sources to obtain information,
5. communicate through media other than print.

WHAT ABOUT THE SYLLABUS?

Many people think the teacher who arrives at school the first day of classes with a syllabus for each class worked out in detail for the first six or eight weeks is a teacher who has things under control. They are right. What the teacher has under control is the students. He or she communicates one message simply by handing out a syllabus on the first day of classes: "This is *MY* course, not *OUR* course! I know where you should be going, and I am going to get you there."

Teachers who adopt the whole-language approach to teaching do not want to control students and do not want to own the courses they teach. They want instead to assess their students' needs and create courses to meet these needs.

This does not mean that these teachers have no standards or that they permit their classrooms to be raucous and disorderly. Nor does it mean that if some students want to sit in class for the whole hour and eat ice

22

cream or blow bubbles with their chewing gum, the teacher will permit it. What we are talking about here is not permissive education. We are talking rather about *responsive education*, an education that is responsive to the real needs of real students rather than to the hypothetical needs of students whom teachers have not yet met and come to know.

It takes sensitive, intuitive teachers to realize what the real needs of their students are and to provide creative environments in which these students can reveal their true natures—which many of them do not themselves realize or acknowledge. Most students are not accustomed to looking into themselves. Rather, they have usually been encouraged to assume the personalities they think their teachers want them to assume. Some of them have lived the lies conventional schools have imposed upon them for so long that they can't distinguish between these lies and truth. As a result, they do not know who they are.

ALLOWING STUDENTS TO GROW

Teachers who use the first three exercises in this book because they are working up to teaching *The Chocolate War* will soon find that the exercises suggest other ideas to them. Perhaps a student has read or heard about Carl Bernstein's *Loyalties: A Son's Memoir*.[3] The book tells about what Bernstein, now an investigative reporter, experienced as he grew up in Washington during World War II and afterward with parents who had belonged to the Communist Party. For their leftist activities, both parents lost their jobs and received widespread negative publicity during the McCarthy era—their son's school years.

Young Carl's classmates were forbidden by their parents to play with this son of Communist parents. Bernstein's book is wholly germane to the questions posed by the exercises, as, for example, are the death dialogues of Socrates, who, when he was sentenced to die for corrupting the youth of Athens, was given the opportunity to escape to another Greek city-state, but declined the opportunity. He believed that citizens must obey, as they exist, laws enacted for the good of the populace in general while trying to change any laws they cannot conscientiously follow because they believe them to be unjust or ineffective.

If society is to be orderly, change, according to Socrates, has to come about through established judicial processes. Not agreeing with a given law does not give one license to disobey it. One or more students might wish to read about Socrates' trial and death in Maxwell Anderson's *Barefoot in Athens*,[4] a play that raises many of the questions these exercises pose.

Students might find it productive to tell what they know about civil disobedience during the Vietnamese conflict or during the student rebellion in China in 1989. A discussion of this topic can lead to some of the following activities.

Exercise 2.4

1. Read Henry Thoreau's essay on civil disobedience or Jerome Lawrence's *The Night Thoreau Spent in Jail*,[5] which is based upon it. Now write a letter from a modern Thoreau to a friend telling why he has decided to serve or not to serve in the army during the Vietnamese conflict.
2. Read *The Night Thoreau Spent in Jail* and *Barefoot in Athens*. What do you think Socrates would have thought of Thoreau? List three things about Thoreau you think Socrates would have appreciated and three that he might not have appreciated.
3. Find an item in your local newspaper or in a weekly news magazine that tells about someone who is defying a law. Either write a letter to the editor about this matter or tape interviews for an "As I See It" column about the situation.
4. Organize a classroom debate on the following statement: "Guilty Is Guilty: If the speed limit is 35 miles an hour, a driver going 36 mph is as guilty of an infraction as a person driving 70 mph." Set this activity up as a formal debate with three people taking the pro and three taking the contra side of the argument.

These activities help students to
1. understand the universality and continuity of ethical problems,
2. examine more than one side of an argument,
3. resolve some of their fundamental ethical dilemmas,
4. devise formal arguments about one side of a controversial issue.

HOW DO WE KNOW WHAT WE KNOW?

Most people take for granted much of what they know. If we stop to think about it, we learned most of the information we possess informally during the first five or six years of our lives, when the need to learn was critical, the thirst to learn unquenchable. We had not lived long before we were forced to make sense of noises that surrounded us; having done this, we began desperately to imitate these noises to the point that we could be understood by people who make similar noises.

We learned some negative lessons that have lasted us a lifetime—not to touch a hot stove, not to pet a growling dog, not to defy anyone bigger and more powerful than we are, not to jump into the deep end of a swimming pool if we cannot swim, not to stick a screwdriver into an electrical socket. And we probably learned a major part of the rest of what we know in relatively informal settings.

A great deal we learned in more formal settings, such as classrooms, we have probably forgotten unless we had to use it on the job after we left school. Probably 90 percent of the facts we learn in school are forgotten in less than 10 years if we do not have occasion to use them.

Most of us, for example, learned the binomial theorem and its proof by the time we were 15. Now—at 30, 45, or 70—we probably cannot dredge up the details of that theorem from our deep recollective wells. We learned the theorem and its proof for a test, we spewed it out when we were expected to do so, and we probably passed the test. Then most of us forgot this something we quite likely would never need to know again.

What learning most of us have done as adults has come to us through the media, particularly radio and television, or through direct contact with other people in social or work settings. In our interactions with other people, everyone talks, no one raises a hand for permission to speak, and neither quiet nor order is enforced, although civil behavior often decrees that only one person speaks at a time.

Ironically, however, the effectiveness of teachers is often judged by their ability to keep their classrooms orderly and their students quiet, even though order and quiet seldom accompany real, vital learning activities. When real learning is going on, it is often accompanied by the hum of busy-ness or by some louder noise. Good teachers will always be able to bring their classes back to order if the need occurs, but their classes will be buzzing with activity much of the time. The activity will be directed at specific learning outcomes, not necessarily for the class, but rather for each student in the class.

MY STUDENTS CAN'T

Some teachers are obsessed by what their students cannot do. They may judge them and gear their teaching to them on this negative basis. In whole-learning programs, teachers—cognizant of the fact that no one can do everything equally well—focus on students' abilities and interests rather than on their disabilities and on curriculum guides. Rudolf Flesch wrote *Why Johnny Can't Read*[6] and launched a thriving enterprise that led to books and articles enumerating other things that Johnny or Juanita could not do. A whole-language teacher might instead have written *But Johnny/Juanita CAN Draw/Sing/Lead People/Fix Motors/Repair Roller Skates/Solve Problems* or anything else that the hypothetical Johnny and Juanita *CAN* do.

We doubt that any of the people reading this book can paint like Vermeer, sing like Caruso, or play tennis like Michael Chang—nor can its authors. We do not, however, feel like second-class citizens because of these deficiencies that some people might even view as disabilities. Rather than cogitate on what they can't do, sensible people find out what they can do, and they do it—at least after they leave school and enter the workplace. If they cannot do mathematics easily, they do not become engineers; if they cannot tell a metaphor from a cow pasture, they do not go into literary studies.

The world does not judge people on their disabilities but rather on what they can do and what they can contribute to society. Schools owe students equal treatment and respect: that is what the whole-language approach promotes.

HOW *DO* I PREPARE TO TEACH MY CLASSES?

Teachers should have some coherent notion of what they hope their students will achieve and of what specific skills they will develop during any grading period, semester, or year. They must have some idea of the sets of books their students will need and of the audiovisual materials they must order for the first months of the term. All these things have to be decided in advance. To arrive in class the first day with a syllabus, however, is to assume a control that is better assumed by the combined efforts of students and teachers, and that is best not put into writing until teachers know something about their students.

If teachers come to class with ideas and exercises on the first day, students will realize that they are not working with someone who is directionless. As these students are brought increasingly into the process of curriculum planning, they will appreciate being able to explore their own interests and to have a hand in determining the directions and procedures of the course. If teachers handle the situation well, courses that are student-oriented will be the ones that students remember positively throughout their lives. These will also be the courses in which students experience their most significant growth.

THE WHOLE-LANGUAGE APPROACH AND SUBJECT MATTER

Whole-language teachers put students before subject matter, which is not a revolutionary arrangement; people, when you come to think of it, have always been more important than things. Putting students first, however, does not mean that subject matter counts for nothing. People function best in life by knowing as much as they can and by developing to the utmost the abilities they have, ever widening their search for knowledge so that they can work toward achieving their highest potentials.

When a whole-language approach is employed properly, it will accelerate the learning processes of students by beginning with things that interest them and mean something to them. Students in such situations will work from their own interests and enthusiasms toward expanding their spheres of interest and developing additional enthusiasms. Given their choices of what to study and how to study it, many people quickly make themselves experts in fields of genuine interest. Many hobbyists have been led into fruitful lifetime vocations related to their hobbies.

Early in a school term, perhaps in the first week, teachers can learn a great deal about their students by having them fill out the following questionnaire.

Exercise 2.5

1. What would you most like to change about yourself? Why would you like to make this change?
2. What would you most like to change about someone who is close to you? Why would you like this person to change?
3. What worries you most? Why do you think it worries you?
4. What would you most hate to lose? Why?
5. If you had a whole month to do anything you wanted to and had a moderate amount of money with which to do it, what would you do? Explain your choice. What does this choice tell you about yourself?
6. What event or occurrence has made you the angriest in recent months? Why do you think you react angrily to this event or occurrence? Consider the underlying reasons for your feelings and reactions.
7. Think of a time when you thought you were treated unfairly. How did you cope with the situation? Would you cope with it the same way now? Why or why not?

8. Think of a time when you treated someone unfairly. What did you do? How did you feel afterward? Did you try to remedy the situation?

These questions will help students to
1. analyze some of their actions and emotions,
2. reveal to another person hidden parts of themselves,
3. move from subjectivity toward objectivity,
4. assess their actions and reactions consciously.

USING REAL-LIFE SITUATIONS

John and Susan Miller live in a small midwestern town on a street of well-kept lawns and neat, carefully maintained houses. They deplore the disappearance of the prairie, and they have allowed native plants to grow in their yard in an attempt to replicate the prairie. Doing this has had two results:
1. the bird population around their house has tripled, and
2. the neighbors have lodged a formal complaint with the town council, calling the Millers' yard a weed patch.

Like many towns, the Millers' community has an ordinance relating to the appearance of one's property. Upon receiving complaints from the Millers' neighbors, the president of the town council drove past the Millers' house and looked at their yard, then sent the Millers a letter explaining to them that their yard is in violation of the law, which specifically states that residents will keep their property as "weed-free as possible and will maintain their yards in a seemly and attractive manner." The Millers are given 30 days to conform, after which they will be liable for a fine of $500, doubling each month, until the situation is remedied.

Susan Miller writes a letter of response to the town council. The gist of her letter is that she and her husband own their property and that it gives them pleasure to replicate the original landscape of the area. She also asks the town council to define the terms "weeds" and "seemly and attractive manner."

The town council does not answer Susan Miller's questions but does call a special meeting 10 days hence at which the Millers and their complaining neighbors will each present their arguments to the council.

28

Exercise 2.6

1. Using any sources you care to, write an answer to Susan Miller's letter in which you respond to her request that the town council define two terms crucial to the town ordinance she and her husband are accused of violating.
2. Do an improvisation that depicts the meeting with the town council. There should be enough parts so that everyone in the class can be involved—six to eight town council members, a lawyer for the town, possibly a lawyer for the Millers or one for their neighbors, the two Millers, an expert witness—a botanist—whom the Millers have brought with them, and as many neighbors as it takes for everyone to have a role.
3. Interview five or six people about the Millers' conflict with the town council and their neighbors, and, using these interviews as a basis, do an "As I See It" column for a newspaper.
4. A national anchorperson for the evening network news has heard about the Millers' situation and thinks it has enough human interest appeal to warrant covering it for the prime time evening news. Make a video- or audiotape of this 150-second (2.5-minute) news spot.
5. Draw an editorial cartoon for your school newspaper in which you depict either the Millers' garden (as they call it), the neighbors, or the special meeting of the town council.
6. Find out whether your town has any ordinances relating to the appearance of residential buildings and the land surrounding them. If it has, bring in a copy of such ordinances and lead a class discussion that focuses on the question of whether and/or how terms in the document are defined.

These activities help students to
1. realize the need to define terms clearly,
2. think about individual rights as opposed to the general welfare of the community,
3. formulate arguments based upon law,
4. differentiate between how a story is covered locally and how the same story is covered nationally.

WHAT ABOUT DISCIPLINE?

The authors are quite aware that discipline problems exist in some schools. In situations where maintaining order is a problem, repressive measures may control the situation temporarily. Students at some stages of development are more likely to pose discipline problems than students of other ages.

Discipline problems are symptomatic of problems students have to cope with and work through. The more severe these problems are, the more difficult it is to maintain an environment in which learning takes place. The whole-language approach, however, helps students to discover themselves, to understand what bothers them and why. If we had any foolproof solution to discipline problems, we could write a book that would sell a million copies almost instantly.

Rather, we must admit that in a society as complex as ours, some students will inevitably cause difficulties, perhaps sufficient to delay the progress of others or to prevent progress in class altogether. The whole-language approach will not work wonders with students who carry the scars of a troubled childhood. It stands a good chance, though, of helping such students realize that perhaps through learning they will find solutions to some of their most pressing problems. They might learn some coping mechanisms by thinking through the kinds of exercises found in a book like this one, perhaps modified specifically to situations like the ones they have to deal with in their daily lives.

Teachers who work in blighted or troubled areas will learn a great deal about their students by doing a neighborhood survey before or shortly after the beginning of school. This means strolling through the neighborhood, talking with people—shopkeepers, street people, children, anyone who will talk with them. They can also listen to people talking among themselves. They might come to understand that typical living arrangements in a given neighborhood do not permit students to do homework assignments or to work on school projects at home.

One of the writers of this book taught in Philadelphia's Black ghetto and was startled when he did a neighborhood survey to discover that the average per-room occupancy in the area his school served was almost five, some of whom slept in shifts. Learning this one fact made him realize that he had to allow class time for his students to work on projects; there was no hope of their being able to do them at home.

He also realized quickly that on some days he could not teach what he was supposed to teach because a rumble had completely dislocated the neighborhood. On such days, it was better to talk about what had happened than to stick doggedly to the lesson plan. This was part of a whole-language approach, although the term had not yet been coined. The approach, arrived at intuitively, dealt with what was on the students' minds.

After a neighborhood murder or drug bust or rumble, we wrote out our feelings, then we talked about the problem. Learning took place, although probably not the specific kind of learning that was anticipated for that day.

Discipline? In many situations, it has to do with repressing people. When repression is replaced with understanding and open communication, discipline begins to take care of itself, although it might not result in a quiet classroom. The writer soon learned that his ghetto students were not accustomed to quiet; for these students, quiet happened only when a police car pulled up outside their buildings. Quiet equalled *THREAT.* Once he learned this important lesson, the writer ceased to take personally the noise that frequently was a part of the learning environment in his classroom. In time, he reached the point of being able to touch the lives of at least some of his students.

A PARTING PROBLEM TO WORK OUT

What would you do if, as happened to the writer on his second day in the ghetto school, the room suddenly became quiet and every student stared at the clock? When the hand finally ticked to the next minute, 35 students each dropped a book on the floor.

Antics like this occur in schools. They can unnerve new teachers—even experienced teachers. The writer was unnerved, but he recovered sufficiently to pick up a large history book and drop it to the floor. He looked at the class and said, "I didn't know we were all going to drop a book. Why didn't you let me in on it? Don't you think I'm a member of this class, too?" That nipped the problem in the bud and taught the writer one important lesson: Don't turn small pranks into federal cases. Deal with them as creatively and humorously as you can. Things will probably straighten themselves out—not overnight, but eventually.

Notes

1. See James Britton, *Language and Learning* (Hammondsworth, U.K.: Penguin Books, 1970). See also Britton, Tony Burgess, Nancy Martin, Alex McLeod, and Harold Rosen, *The Development of Writing Abilities, 11–18* (London: Macmillan, 1975), and Janet Emig, *The Composing Processes of Twelfth*

Graders (Urbana, Ill.: National Council of Teachers of English, 1971). Emig differentiates between *reflexive* writing, similar to Britton's expressive writing, and *extensive* writing, similar to Britton's transactional writing.

2. Robert E. Cormier, *The Chocolate War* (New York: Pantheon, 1974). Pantheon reprinted this book in 1986. It is readily available.
3. Carl Bernstein, *Loyalties: A Son's Memoir* (New York: Simon and Schuster, 1989).
4. Maxwell Anderson, *Barefoot in Athens* (New York: Sloane, 1951).
5. Jerome Lawrence, *The Night Thoreau Spent in Jail*. First published in 1970, this is most easily available in the Bantam edition published in 1988.
6. Rudolf Flesch, *Why Johnny Can't Read* (New York: Harper and Row, 1955). This book has been reprinted frequently and is easily obtainable.

Chapter 3

THE SKILLS OF DECODING: LISTENING AND READING

Listening is the first language skill children master. It is a skill of decoding. The code initially is mere noise to the small baby who hears it, but as babies grow into children, they become more skillful at detecting patterns in the noise around them. They begin to decode it, to know what it means. This is their first major step toward literacy.

Teachers, particularly high school teachers, usually spend little or no class time teaching their students how to listen. They assume their students can listen when they come to high school; most elementary school teachers make the same assumption, although such an assumption may not be justified by the evidence. To hear and to understand is not quite the same as to listen in a sophisticated way that leads to productive academic outcomes.

The decoding skill that high school teachers most often concentrate on is reading. No matter what subjects they teach, all teachers are in some degree reading teachers. Students who are generally proficient readers do not necessarily have equal proficiency in reading the array of printed matter they encounter in a typical school day. For example, the sports page of the newspaper is easier reading for most of them than a chapter in a history book or an instruction manual in chemistry lab.

High school teachers who assume their students are proficient in reading often find within the first few days of class that this assumption is incorrect. Such a discovery can be unsettling to beginning teachers, but they might view it as a challenge rather than as something to be upset over. Teachers, therefore, need to know some of the basic principles of reading instruction. They need to have ideas about reading and a supply of easily implemented exercises they can use with their students when necessary.

HOW MUCH DOES THE AVERAGE PERSON READ?

Many people nowadays seem not to read much. You probably know people who haven't read a book in years and who are dependent primarily on the television set or the radio for whatever current information they receive. Perhaps as you think back over the last week, you will conclude that you haven't done much reading during that time.

We all know that sitting in an overstuffed armchair with a book in our hands and our eyes on the book appears to be reading. We would also have to allow that reading the newspaper or the *TV Guide* or *Time* magazine is reading, although it is reading of a different kind from reading a novel or a textbook. To find out what reading is and how much reading you do, consider the exercises that follow.

Exercise 3.1

1. Write your definition of reading. You might wish to begin with a dictionary definition, but this is just a first step toward arriving at your own workable definition.
2. In a notebook, make a notation every time you read. What you count as reading will depend upon the definition you arrived at in Item 1. Include the time and the type of reading you did. Make careful entries for two hours during the day, perhaps the first hour you are awake and another hour in the middle of the day. This assignment sounds easy; just carry a notebook around with you and make a notation every time you read. Of course, in order to do this, you must decide what kinds of reading to count.

These activities help students to
1. devise a personal definition of a key word, stated in their own terms;
2. reconsider a definition they had always taken for granted;
3. analyze one of their own major behaviors;
4. develop skill in notetaking.

As students work toward defining a word like *reading*, they begin to realize that reading words on a page is not the only kind of reading people do. They quickly have to acknowledge that although reading a highway billboard is different from reading the comic strip and that reading the comic strip is different from reading editorials, all these activities are, quite legitimately, designated *reading*.

No quarrel so far. The activities just mentioned are clearly reading according to most dictionary definitions of the word. No lexicographer would define reading by making such a value judgment as, "Reading takes place only when one is assimilating quality literature." But what about the airline pilot who says to the control tower, "I read you" or the fortune teller who says, "I read trouble in her tea leaves"?

To arrive at a broader definition of reading, let's start at the very beginning of a typical day. We snort a little, roll over in bed, and glance bleary-eyed at the clock beside it. It is 6:37 a.m. Great! We can sleep another 23 minutes. Even though we are about to get a few extra winks, we have committed our first reading act of the day. We read the clock! If it was a digital clock, we read the numbers. If it was an older clock, we read the position of the hands and the numbers they pointed to.

In either case, we assimilated necessary information through our eyes (read what time it was) and acted on that information (rolled over and went back to sleep). Many people would accept this as a definition of reading: Reading occurs when people assimilate information through their eyes and act upon it.

Exercise 3.2

1. Read the definition of reading given above. Indicate in writing how much of it you accept. What problems do you see in it? How would you alter it to arrive at your own definition?
2. Form groups of five or six students, all of whom have their own written answers to Item 1. Each student will read his or her responses to Item 1, then the group will work toward arriving at its own definition of *reading.* This exercise should be limited to 15 minutes. Have each group appoint a spokesperson to present its definition.
3. Each spokesperson will present to the class the definition agreed upon by his or her group, including some of the arguments advanced within the group in favor of that definition. Members of the class will then have five minutes to ask questions of the group.

These activities help students to
1. argue from the standpoint of definition,
2. transform personal written notes into part of a group document,
3. listen carefully to a presentation and ask questions about it,
4. assess the elements that keep a definition from being wholly valid.

From seven until eight o'clock, most early risers become reading demons. They get into the shower and turn the hot and cold faucets. In order to get the mix of water they need, they probably read them by their positions rather than by the words stamped on them. In a sense, they read their closets and bureau drawers to get from them the clothing they will wear for the day.

Then they go to breakfast. They decide on the kind of cereal they want and take the box from the cupboard. Something related to reading enables them to get just the box they want. It is hard to say exactly how they achieve this feat, but somehow they achieve it. Maybe they read the actual words on the box that tell them the brand name. More likely, however, they read the size, shape, and color combinations before them, enabling them to pull from the shelf exactly what cereal boxes they want. If they are diet conscious, they might read the side of a box to determine fat or protein content or the number of calories each serving has. They read the milk cartons in the refrigerator in some way so that they do not end up with heavy cream or buttermilk on their cereal.

The chances are that they flip through the morning paper, read closely the parts that interest them most, skim the parts that interest them least, and scan the classified ads or department store ads looking for key words or phrases like "cream-puff condition" or "low mileage" or "like new" or "XJE" or "SALE" or "bargain" or "up to 50% discounts" that will tell them which ads deserve their closer attention. It is clear that people do not read all the printed matter they encounter in the same way.

Next they might glance at a letter or memorandum they have to read in preparation for something they plan to do early in the day. They read the note under the magnetized plum on the refrigerator door reminding them they have a dental appointment at 10:30.

Finally it is time to leave the house. They rush out to their cars, where some real reading begins because all the gauges before them offer written information—alphabetical, numerical, or pictorial. Perhaps, then, reading can be defined as any graphic display that communicates information, although that definition, because of the word *graphic* is too narrow to include all the reading activities mentioned above.

The minute our hypothetical drivers pull into the street, they have imposed upon them another form of reading; they read the traffic patterns they are dealing with; they read all the road signs and street signs that help to warn and direct them. Many of the road signs are pictorial, sometimes accompanied by words, sometimes not. It soon becomes obvious that to record a day's reading is quite a consuming task. Doing so, however, will

1. force people to define what reading is, and

2. make them realize that by most definitions of reading, people read more each day than they think they do.

Because people are more dependent upon listening than upon reading and because they listen much more than they read, using even the broadest definition of reading, it would be all but impossible to keep an accurate record of all that we read in even a given minute.

Sound is much more pervasive than material that falls into whatever definition of reading you have arrived at. People are exposed to inter-mixtures of sound all the time, hearing someone talk but simultaneously hearing the wind blow outside, the tree branches scrape against the roof, the hum of the refrigerator, the faint sounds of music from down the block, the sounds of trucks and automobiles accelerating or squealing their wheels on the street outside. Listening, like reading, is a decoding activity.

UNDERSTANDING DETAILED INFORMATION

We receive a great deal of information orally. If those who speak are unclear or give more detail than listeners can assimilate, the communication of the information is flawed. If listeners are inattentive or if they cannot remember all the details of what is being communicated, they cannot use the information they receive.

Exercise 3.3

1. Go up to someone you do not know either in your school or in a public place like a shopping mall or service station. Ask that person for directions to get to a well-known location some distance away that is not in a straight line from where you are. Record the directions you are given on a cassette. Now go to a second person who has not seen you talking with the first person, and ask for the same directions, recording them as well. Compare the clarity and effectiveness of both sets of directions. Write a brief paper or give a brief classroom presentation in which you analyze the reason one set of directions was clearer than the other.
2. Write directions that tell a peer who does not know where you live, how to get from the school to your home. Then ask a second student who does know where you live to tell the first student how to get from the school to your house or apartment.
3. Students should work in pairs on this exercise. One student will write directions that tell how to do something like make a sand-

wich or draw a picture of a bird or an apple. This student will then read the directions slowly to the other student, who will follow them precisely. Have several pairs of students do this exercise in front of the class. If the student following the directions does not succeed in accomplishing what the first student had in mind, get the class to figure out why the outcome was flawed. How might the directions be altered to result in the desired outcome?

4. Have each student bring in a set of directions for putting something together or for performing some procedure on a computer. Have students work in groups of five or six to compare their sets of directions. Ask each group to select the directions they think are least clear. For the next day, hand out ditto sheets reproducing the unclear directions and ask each group to rewrite one or more sets of directions to increase their clarity.

5. Have each student find two sets of directions for performing an identical process—baking a chocolate cake, changing an oil filter, tuning a guitar, adjusting a humidifier for winter. Ask all students to write a paper or make a classroom presentation in which they compare and contrast the two sets of directions, indicating clearly which set they prefer and telling precisely why they prefer it.

These activities help students to
1. realize the need for clarity,
2. analyze what makes directions clear or unclear,
3. use comparison and contrast as rhetorical devices,
4. develop techniques of oral inquiry and presentation.

GETTING YOURSELF FROM HERE TO THERE

For this activity, teachers will need maps and timetables. A few road atlases would help. Possibly the local branch of a major automobile club could be persuaded to contribute sets of road maps to the school. Timetables from the local bus company and from long distance bus lines will be useful, as will those from railways and airlines. All these materials provide quite complicated reading challenges to students, but they are exactly the kinds of materials that people frequently have to deal with in real-life situations.

Exercise 3.4

1. You want to visit a place at least 300 miles from your home, making the drive in one day. You want to take as scenic a route as possible, using interstate highways as little as you can. On a sheet of paper, write the name of the town you are starting from. Write a complete routing for your trip, noting distances. You plan to leave in the early morning and you estimate you will average 42.5 miles an hour, including all stops. You want to make fuel and/or comfort stops approximately every hour and a half. You plan to eat lunch in a restaurant sometime around 12:15. On your paper, beneath the name of your starting point indicate the following:

   a. The name of each major city or town you pass through.
   b. The distance from each town to the next town.
   c. The names of the towns you plan to stop in with anticipated arrival times.
   d. The route numbers of the roads you will be traveling.
   e. Indications of where you have to change routes. Mark each of these places with a large arrow.
   f. The estimated arrival time at your destination.
   g. The total number of miles covered.

2. Using this information, how much should you spend on fuel if your car averages 28.4 miles a gallon in highway driving and if the average cost of gasoline is estimated to be $1.13 a gallon? Explain in writing how you arrived at your answer.

3. Using only public transportation, plan a trip from your home to a point at least 500 miles away, leaving on Saturday morning as soon after nine as possible. Refer to the timetables in the reading corner, and draw up a clearly written schedule for your trip. Be sure to indicate any changes of vehicles. Be sure also that all the public transportation you plan to use runs on Saturdays.

4. You are planning your first trip to Europe and will be away 21 days. You want to divide your time equally between England, Germany, and Italy. Using the airline schedules in the reading corner, plan a trip, leaving the United States on Friday night, March 2, and leaving Italy to return home on Thursday morning, March 22. Include all auxiliary transportation such as connecting flights, buses, or limousines to the the airport.

These activities help students to
1. work effectively with the kinds of printed material people often use in their daily lives,
2. incorporate mathematical skills into language arts situations,
3. present information in schedule (outline) form,
4. interpret symbols in timetables to make sure that the transportation they need runs on the day they need it.

THE SKILLS WE TAKE FOR GRANTED

Teachers always make assumptions about students and their abilities before they meet them on the first day of class. A necessary part of curriculum planning, such assumptions usually are reasonably accurate. Sometimes, however, they are inaccurate, and sometimes teachers are baffled when students do not perform according to the expectations they have formed from their assumptions. When this happens, the danger exists of diagnosing the situation incorrectly. An incorrect diagnosis can result in using an ineffective remedy or trying no remedy at all.

Let us say that three or four students in class have difficulty understanding what they read. In conference the teacher finds out that they do not understand some of the key words they encounter in books. The solution seems easy: Tell them to keep a dictionary nearby when they read and to use it when they need to. Good advice, but as week follows week, the condition persists. The teacher's diagnosis? Laziness.

Perhaps that would be your diagnosis, too. When they reach this conclusion, teachers nag their students a little, and if no improvement occurs, some of them give up on these students, considering them hopeless and feeling defeated by that assumption. In doing so, they are overlooking a fundamental possibility that might explain the problem and help students to eradicate it.

The one thing the teacher has not found out in this case is *why* the students are not using their dictionaries. Students who do not know the sequence of letters in the alphabet cannot use dictionaries efficiently. Some high school students, regardless of their ability, do not know the alphabet. This is a fact they are reluctant and embarrassed to admit. At their age, they presume they are supposed to know the alphabet and they feel dumb if they don't know it.

Not knowing the alphabet limits students in many ways. It makes it difficult for them to use dictionaries as well as to use indexes in books, to use the card catalog in the library, and to engage effectively in any activity in which alphabetizing is important.

Exercise 3.5

1. Using a black magic marker, write a different word on each of 10 cards, making sure that at least three of the words begin with the same letter (*romance, ruthless, rent*) and that at least one set has several of its beginning letters in common (*ransack/ranger/ransom*). Give a card to each of the first 10 students who come through the door. When the class has settled down, have the 10 students with cards come to the front of the room and arrange themselves in alphabetical order. Ask the class to discuss how they knew where words like *ransack, ranger,* and *ransom* should go.
2. On the chalkboard, write the following list of words or one like it:

fence	rent
machine	possibility
episode	which
crying	wages
wrench	cryptogram
earning	

   Make sure that at least two or three of the words begin with the same letter and that one pair has several of the initial letters in common (*crying/cryptogram* above). Ask your students to arrange these words in alphabetical order.
3. Obtain from your school or local librarian a stack of discarded cards from the card catalog. You should have 300–500 of these cards to do this exercise. You can use them over every year. Give each student five to ten cards, and have them alphabetize them as fast as they can.

These activities help students to
1. learn how to arrange items by their beginning letters,
2. learn how to make fine distinctions if several beginning letters are the same,
3. understand why they must sometimes make even finer distinctions,
4. make kinesthetic connections with letters and words.

USING THE PARTS OF A BOOK

By the time they get to high school, students are used to books, but they do not always know how to use them. Students should work on some discovery exercises on using books before they begin to write anything like resource papers. Students cannot hope to be able to use the library effectively until they know how to use books effectively. For the exercises suggested below, it is best to use textbooks your students are familiar with, preferably from some of their other classes.

Exercise 3.6

1. Using a textbook from another class and no other source, find as much of the following information as you can, indicating on what page of the book the information was given:
   a. What is the copyright date?
   b. When was the author born?
   c. How many chapters does the book have?
   d. Under what card catalog headings would you find this book?
   e. Is this the first edition of the book?
   f. In what chapter of the book would you find information about...? (Select a topic from the table of contents.)
   g. On what specific pages would you find information about...? (Select an item from the index that gives several page references.)
2. Study the following portion of an index from a cookbook and answer the questions that follow the selection.

Mulberries, preserving 317
Mullet, filleting 614–615
Mulligatawny 221
Mush, corn meal 187–189
    and bacon 287
    baked 187
    grinding 187
    fried..188
Mussels, cleaning 724
Mushrooms 429–441
    and haddock, creamed 616
    breaded 437
    french fried..431

a. Which items do not have to do directly with cooking?
b. Which items seem out of place? Why?
c. Which item(s) are out of alphabetical order?
d. Are any of the words above unfamiliar to you? If so, write them down and look up their definitions.
e. Which items have to do with things that are done before cooking?
f. Put check marks beside the items that probably contain no meat.
g. Near what page would you look if you wanted to make a broccoli quiche? Why?
h. Near what page would you look if you wanted a shrimp recipe? Why?
i. Near what pages would you look if you wanted to make creamed spinach soup? Why?

3. Find a book that has footnotes or endnotes. Examine these notes and classify them under descriptive headings that you devise. These headings should indicate the different functions that various notes serve.
4. What generalizations can you reach about the way foototes or endnotes are structured? How does a reference to a book or article in one of these notes differ from an entry in the bibliography for the same book or article?

The activities help students to
1. test and enhance their alphabetizing skills,
2. understand how material is organized for indexing,
3. draw inferences from material in indexes,
4. classify information by function,
5. use a dictionary effectively.

READING DURING SCHOOL HOURS

In the course of any school day, students use books and other print media regularly in all their subject-matter classes. Using books is important, but *using* a book is different from *reading* a book. We *use* the telephone directory but do not *read* it the way we read a Reynolds Price novel or Eudora Welty short story.

Some teachers are hesitant to allow their students to read for fun in class, thinking that precious class time will be wasted if students are just sitting at their desks reading. Nothing, however, is farther from the truth. Some students will never engage in recreational reading if they don't do it in class.

Sustained Silent Reading (SSR) programs have been around for several decades. In such programs, teachers set aside a specific time every day or every other day or every week for everyone in class to read something of his or her own choosing. Both students and teachers read anything they care to read. They are encouraged to bring something with them they want to read, but if they fail to do this, teachers usually have a variety of books in the room from which they can make their selections. The time allotted to SSR can range from 15 or 20 minutes once a day to a full class period once a week.

Some schools have instituted reading periods for the whole school. Everyone in the school—students, teachers, guidance counselors, administrators, secretaries, and other staff—reads during the reading period. Such programs help to convince students that reading is important enough to warrant using some of the school day to do it. Students who have never been avid readers may soon discover that if they are reading something that interests them, reading is a pleasurable and rewarding activity.

Some resourceful teachers have promoted reading in their classrooms by setting up reading corners for students to use when they have finished their other work. They stock reading corners with paperback books, magazines, newspapers, catalogs, how-to-do-it manuals, driver's license manuals, travel literature, and anything else that interests members of the class. Students are urged to bring in material for these reading centers, and doing so makes them feel they have a real stake in classroom reading.

Sometimes teachers can persuade the media specialist to check out a cart full of books that can remain in the classroom for two to four weeks so that students always have something to read when they have nothing else to do. One imaginative teacher in North Carolina took a large piece of colorful felt and sewed a dozen felt pockets, each in a contrasting color, to it. She hung this construction on a wall in the front of her room and filled each pocket with a used paperback book. She invited students to bring in their old paperbacks, saying that they could take any book they wanted to read from one of the pockets, but they had to replace it with one they had finished reading and were willing to let someone else have. Teachers who use this technique need to have a supply of old paperbacks so that they can replace any books students might put into a pocket that would be morally or otherwise offensive to people in the community.

WHERE DOES SUSTAINED SILENT READING LEAD?

Once students get used to SSR, they like it and want it to continue. The outcomes from such a program can be substantial, but effective teachers build on SSR to enhance the positive outcomes of the process. One way to do this is to ask students to complete recommendation sheets for every book or story they read during the time reserved for SSR. The sheets should be filed in the classroom so that other students can have access to them when they are trying to decide on what their next readings will be.

Exercise 3.7

Fill in the form that follows (Figure 1) for every book you read during our free reading periods. Be as complete as you can. Your audience is your classmates, many of whom will decide to read or not to read a book based on what you have said. (Some personal opinion is acceptable in these reviews, but teachers should urge reviewers to remain objective.)

This activity helps students to
  1. identify an audience,
  2. write to a stipulated audience,
  3. employ critical judgment,
  4. learn more about an author's work.

Your Name: _____

Author's Last Name: _____ First Name: _____

Title of book: _____

Place and date of publication: _____

Did you enjoy this book? Why or why not?

What kinds of people do you think would get the most out of this book?

Very briefly, summarize the book:

Did you find any of the language or situations in the book offensive? Yes__ No__ Elaborate if you wish.

Do you know of any other books this author has written? If so, give their titles:

Figure 1

IT'S OK TO HATE A BOOK

SSR can lead to valuable outcomes other than the book review indicated above. It is vital that students react to what they read. Their lives will be much fuller if they learn to derive excitement from reading because reading forces them to do the kinds of imaging that a medium like television or film does for them. The transaction between readers and books is a much more intimate one than that between viewers and television shows or films. Readers are active; viewers are generally passive.

Books can excite students positively or negatively. Students often think they are supposed to like everything they read, especially if they read it in school, possibly at the direction of their teachers. They have to know quite early that it is all right to hate a book, but it is as important to understand why we hate a book as it is to know why we love one. Both reactions have to be based upon some sort of valid criteria.

One way to encourage students to be excited by books is to tell them that in the course of a given period—say two months—all students will give brief oral reports on each of two books they have read. Make sure they know they may give a report about a book they hated and tell why they hated it as well as give a report about a book they particularly liked. Suggest a form that each student should follow, such as the one described in Exercise 3.8.

Exercise 3.8

1. Tell the class about the best novel you have read during our SSR periods. Be sure to do the following:
   a. Write the author's name on the board with date of birth and, if the author is not living, death.
   b. Write on the board the full title of the book, including a subtitle if it has one.
   c. List all major characters by name with a brief identification (the father, the clerk, etc.).
   d. List the locale(s) of the book.
   e. Write down the time(s) the story took place.

   After you have written these items on the chalkboard, limit your oral presentation to ten minutes. Set a timer to go off after nine minutes. Make sure that you tell
   a. What you think the author is trying to accomplish.
   b. How the author goes about accomplishing it.

    c.   How the author shows (rather than tells) what each charac-
         ter is like.
    d.   What the book is about—not plot summary, but a statement
         of no more than 25 words that tells what the book is about.
    e.   What elements in the book caused you to enjoy reading it.
2. Using the general forms given above, but omitting from them
   any items that seem inappropriate, tell about the best nonfiction
   book you have read during our SSR periods.
3. Using the forms given above, but omitting from them any items
   that seem inappropriate, tell about a book you read during our
   SSR periods that you did not like, and try to determine what it
   was about the book that made you not like it.
4. Keeping in mind the forms given above and using those parts
   that seem appropriate, tell about a book you have read during
   our SSR periods that you think you might not have understood.
   Indicate why you think you did not understand it, and invite other students in class who have read the book to discuss it with
   you and the class. You lead the discussion.

This activity helps students to
   1. analyze extended works of literature,
   2. differentiate between plot and theme,
   3. solicit the insights of others to understand a book,
   4. understand their positive and negative feelings about a book.

THE CRITICS SELDOM AGREE

Once students have begun to assess literature (including film and drama) and have applied a set of critical criteria to it, they should be encouraged to read what critics have to say about books, films, or plays
they are familiar with. Weekly news magazines contain current reviews,
as do newspapers, especially the Sunday editions of large metropolitan
newspapers.

Students should be encouraged to read (and bring into class) several
reviews of a single book, film, or play. Reviews of a single film may
range from utter condemnation ("A sophomoric effort that insults the
intelligence of filmgoers") to ecstatic praise ("If this film does not cop
Oscars for its script, its direction, and the superb performances its leading performers bring to it, something is badly amiss in Tinsel Town!").

Anyone who reads such disparate reviews would wonder whether each reviewer had seen the same film. Such disparities, however, are common. From analyzing the reasons for them, students can help to sharpen their own critical apparatus.

Most public and many school libraries have copies of annual volumes that reproduce representative reviews from which students can come to appreciate the broad spectrum of opinion about specific works. The sources that follow are among the most useful for this purpose.

For book reviews:

Book Review Digest. New York: H. W. Wilson Company. This collection of book reviews has been published annually since 1905 and is the one most likely to be in small libraries.

Contemporary Literary Criticism. Detroit: Gale Research Company. The frequently released volumes of this series reproduce a broad range of reviews from popular and scholarly sources.

Twentieth-Century Literary Criticism. Detroit: Gale Research Company. The reviews in this set are similar to those in the immediately preceding volume but they cover works by a broader spectrum of authors.

For theater reviews:

New York Theatre Critics' Review. New York: Critics' Theatre Reviews, Inc. Published annually since 1940, the volumes in this series cover every play on Broadway during a given season, presenting the whole of most major newspaper reviews of a play.

The New York Times Theatre Reviews. New York: Times Books. The volumes in this series contain the *New York Times'* reviews of Broadway plays from 1920 to the present. The series is limited in that it contains no reviews outside the *Times*.

For film reviews:

Film Review Annual. Englewood, N.J.: Film Review Publications. The annual volumes in this series cover all significant films in a given year from 1981 to the present.

Exercise 3.9

1. Read at least five reviews of a single film, play, or book. Write a brief paper that tells how the reviewers differ from each other in what they have written.
2. Write a review of a film or play you have seen recently or of a book you have read. Then, read at least three professional reviews of the same work. How does your review differ from those

you have just read? How do they differ from each other? Which reviewer's opinion is closest to yours? Farthest from yours?

3. Find a student who has recently read a book you have read or seen a film you have seen. Discuss this book or film with each other in front of the class much as Siskel and Ebert discuss films on their television show. It would be best to prepare for this discussion by writing down major points you want to make.

4. Locate at least five reviews of a famous writer's first book or of a very early one—Ernest Hemingway's *In Our Time* (1924), Pearl S. Buck's *East Wind, West Wind* (1930), John Steinbeck's *Cup of Gold* (1929), Reynolds Price's *A Long and Happy Life* (1962), Eudora Welty's *Delta Wedding* (1946; first novel preceded by collections of short stories), Langston Hughes's *The Weary Blues* (1926; a collection of poems), or any other author of your choice. Compare and contrast these early assessments of the writer's work with the same author's later literary reputation.

These activities help students to
1. realize that aesthetic judgments often are not in agreement,
2. discover that early assessments of artists are sometimes not accurate,
3. use comparison and contrast as rhetorical devices,
4. write from both print and nonprint sources,
5. find and use resources for research.

STUDENTS HELPING STUDENTS

Students do their best work when they realize they are in some way accountable for it. If their sole accountability is to their teachers, their obligation to do well will be less than it is if they are accountable to a broader audience.

In high schools there are generally some students who have difficulty reading and some who read very well. These schools can accomplish a great deal if they have their good readers help their less able students learn how to read.

In order to carry out this activity, teachers need to get those students who read well to work with those who read less well or to arrange for them to work with another teacher's students who have reading difficulties.

Exercise 3.10

1. Students who read well need to find out what those with reading problems are reading. Then, they will read into a cassette recorder as well as they can one or more stories that their less able schoolmates are expected to read. They should read slowly and clearly. Once they have done this, each cassette will be made available to students who need it. They will turn the cassette on and begin reading along with it. Soon, they will turn the volume completely down, but continue to read for two or three minutes. Then they will turn the volume up to see whether they are ahead of or behind the reader on the tape.

2. Students who volunteer to read stories will write a study guide for each story they read. This study guide will be reproduced on a photocopying machine and given to students who listen to the cassette to use before they read their stories. Study guides can be of many sorts. A typical one might look something like this:

Title of story: _____

Author, including name and dates: _____

What is the story about?

Five words you might have trouble with:
(List five problem words and their definitions.)

Other words in the story that might baffle you:
(List any other problem words you might have to look up in a dictionary.)

Reader's name: _____

_____

These activities help students to
1. determine what vocabulary might cause problems,
2. work together toward achieving learning objectives,
3. develop skill in oral reading (the reader making the cassette) and in silent reading (the reader using the cassette),
4. accept responsibility for teaching/learning reading.

GETTING THE MOST FROM A CATALOG

Your reading corner should contain catalogs from various stores. For this exercise, students will have a hypothetical amount of money to spend; their aim is to spend as much of it as they can without exceeding their limits. You can learn a great deal about your students' values from their choices.

Exercise 3.11

1. You have $200 to spend on a mail order from any one catalog in the reading corner. You want to spend it on one of the following:
   a. equipment to go skiing
   b. equipment to go scuba diving
   c. accessories for your new bedroom, which already has the basic furniture (bed, chest of drawers, table, desk, etc.)
   d. a back-to-school wardrobe
   e. Christmas shopping
   f. computer accessories
   g. motorbike accessories
   Write a letter or fill in an order form to order what you want to buy, remembering that you cannot exceed $200. Be sure to include the cost of postage and insurance (your catalog will give this information) and of state tax (6.5 percent in your state).
2. Your order arrives, but one item in the parcel is not what you ordered. Rather, it is a much less expensive item that you do not want. Write a letter in which you explain this problem to the company that sent your order. Be sure to include your return address in the proper place and the date.
3. Acting on behalf of the company that sent the order, write a response to the letter in Item 2, suggesting specifically how the matter can best be handled.

This activity helps students to
1. make buying decisions when they use catalogs;
2. stay within a budget;
3. determine the actual cost of what they are ordering, not just the base price;
4. depict clearly a problem that arises;
5. respond specifically to a complaint.

The activities in this chapter engage students in real-life experiences. Teachers might ask whether they will prepare their students for the kinds of tests that high school students have to take. The answer is that not everything we do in the classroom prepares students for tests. These activities cause students to use the skills of decoding—listening and reading—effectively. Doing this will ultimately make them better readers and listeners. These skills carry over into everything they do, including test-taking.

Teachers will notice some overlap in this chapter. Some of the activities demand skills of encoding—speaking and writing—as well as skills of decoding. Any authentic whole-language approach necessarily has overlap. Whole language is what its name suggests. Teachers adopting such an approach will not be able to fence off discrete areas of the communicative skills and isolate them from other areas of those skills.

The writers hope that teachers who read this chapter that focuses on decoding will use it as a pad from which to launch their own exercises. We are flattered when teachers use our material exactly as we have presented it, but students will react best to your teaching if you update and adapt our exercises to the realities of the situations in which you teach.

Chapter 4

THE SKILLS OF ENCODING:
SPEAKING AND WRITING

The beginning of each new school year affords teachers the opportunity to change their language arts classrooms. Sometimes, however, that opportunity is lost. Too often teachers return to school to teach last year's syllabus, with its list of skills prescribed by legislators and education committees, to groups of students who closely resemble the students who walked out the door three months earlier. The lessons have not changed, the students have not changed, nor has the tedium of performing an endless review of the same material. The new academic year, nevertheless, provides the perfect moment to effect change in the high school. A new crop of students has been matriculated, and, not knowing the patterns that have previously existed, can be willing (although unknowing) participants in innovation and experimentation. Likewise, each returning class is faced with unknown challenges—advanced algebra, advanced composition, biology, botany, computer science, chemistry, debate, drama, economics, earth science, chemistry, debate, drama, economics, earth science, French, fuel injector repair, geology, geometry, home economics, history. Students can be introduced to and instructed in these areas of study using pedagogies that not only relieve teachers' boredom, but that create classrooms in which students can learn alongside their teachers, thus making schools exciting and stimulating rather than grim symbols of compulsory attendance laws. An active rather than passive learning environment is what the whole-language approach to communication strives to create.

WHO ARE HIGH SCHOOL WRITERS?

High school writers are, not surprisingly, ninth graders, tenth graders, eleventh graders, and twelfth graders. But, more important, high school writers are students in every class, not just students in English courses. They are also students with myriad social, ethnic, political, and economic backgrounds, who have diverse skills and burning interests and enthusiasms. No two high school writers are the same. Still the situations in which they are sometimes required to write assume a homogeneity that probably does not exist.

WRITING IS A SOCIAL PROCESS

Writing has typically been presented in high schools as an activity that is engaged in singly, that produces "finished" texts within 50-minute periods, that uses rigidly prescribed forms (i.e., five-paragraph themes), and that, by natural or divine order, is boring. Writing is *none* of these things.

Common sense and much research have affirmed the myth of the solitary writer to be just that: a myth. Rarely, if ever, do people write in a vacuum. Writers need other people to talk to, to run their ideas past, to critique their work, to suggest new ideas, and even to provide an occasional diversion.[1] Students, however, often are not allowed to experience writing situations that acknowledge these needs and provide opportunities to meet them. Writing is a social act, performed for social reasons; although a letter is obviously created for real readers, a typical "formal theme" is not—nor does it really have the power to affect society as other forms of writing can do because these other forms reflect real writing situations and actual social needs.[2]

Artists create in ways similar to those writers employ. They engage consciously in a process to produce a finished product. Writers are artists; their composing process consists of many parts including prewriting activities, drafting, revising, editing, and publishing. These steps generally move toward a finished product. Along the way, however, they surface and resurface, as writers decide they need to rethink problems, try other ways of saying something, move the pieces around, or simply start over.[3]

Writing in most language arts situations does not encourage student writers to proceed through this natural process of creation. Instead, teachers frequently require students to limit their invention time to a few minutes before they are asked to produce a draft that is deemed "finished" because it is turned in for evaluation at the end of the class period. This approach to writing leads to several detrimental results:

1. Writing is presented as an art that requires little thought and little time, and is valid only if it is produced within highly structured modes (process analysis, comparison-contrast, description, etc.).
2. Students think writing equals conforming to conventions of usage and mechanics, which they generally erroneously call "grammar."

(Errors are marked and grades assigned based on the frequency of such errors. Much one-shot writing is either thin on content because students get all their commas in the right places, or conventionally a mess because the writers have struggled to say what they need to say and have not had time to polish their mechanics.)

3. Students do not want to write because they assume their writing will not be taken seriously as writing, but as an assessment of their grammatical conformity. Thus, they will not take the necessary risks or make the personal investment required to create effective writing.

4. Teachers become frustrated because their students do not have interesting things to say and show few signs of conforming to convention. They often adopt a teaching attitude that communicates to their students that they don't expect them to write well.

PRODUCTIVE WRITING, FUN WRITING, REAL WRITING

High school grading periods—six to nine weeks in most cases—provide perfect time spans for students to complete projects that involve not only *them* as writers, but also involve groups as writers and entire classes as collaborators.[4] Projects that require students to work with each other illustrate that writing is a social activity, but also reflect many of the actual writing situations people face daily on the job—as members of committees, as individuals responsible for parts of a larger whole, as collaborators on group undertakings. These situations demand specific skills that few people have been exposed to or allowed to practice before they have been forced to deal with them in the workplace.

Teachers who are interested in having students experience working/communicating as parts of groups might start the year by expressing an interest in their organizing a business. We will model the project on the opening of a horse farm because most students know something about horses or are interested in businesses. (We understand that this assignment will not work well in an inner-city setting where horses are almost as rare as dinosaurs, so we offer this project only as a model. An inner-city project might focus on acquiring and transforming a vacant lot into a recreational area or some comparable project.) An initial writing assignment to determine what useful knowledge is available among the group might include the questions given in the following exercise.

Exercise 4.1

1. What do you think we need to look into first as we begin to plan our horse farm? Why is this information important, and what do you know about the subject?
2. People often overlook some essential question when they plan a big project. What question(s) do you foresee that other members of the group may overlook? Why do we need to consider this/these question(s)?
3. What skill do you bring to this project? Why is it important?

These activities help students to
1. be less egocentric as they assess the needs of a group,
2. think through their own knowledge and experience,
3. critique the importance of data,
4. formulate convincing arguments,
5. experience being a valued member of a group.

Written and oral responses to the first exercise usually identify some of the major issues to be addressed at the outset:

- What is the best available land for the site?
- What buildings are needed?
- What types and number of horses are needed?

Many other areas need to be mentioned, however. Students who frequently do not participate in the classroom discussion often point these out. A student reared on a farm may understand the need to provide for veterinary services. A student with an interest in automobiles may realize the need for the purchase of a truck and trailers. A student familiar with computers may understand the computer's ability to keep track of the complicated bloodlines of livestock in a breeding program. These students bring other important issues before the group. Such participation involves and empowers *all* students in the classroom, and improves the effectiveness of the enterprise as well.

Following the discussion of the first writing assignment, another activity can be presented based on a questionnaire like the one that follows.

Exercise 4.2

Thoroughbred Enterprises

For the success of our project we need to have you work in areas that interest you, in areas you know about, and in areas you would like to learn about. In order to help us create teams that focus on doing research and making recommendations, please consider the following target areas:

Land Needs	Ecological Impact
Livestock	Cost Cutting
Business Licenses	Office Needs
Breeding Practices	Insurance
Interior Design	Construction
Building Needs	Utility Needs
Medical Needs	Advertising
Transportation	

1. Identify the areas in which you would be most interested in working. Explain why you would be an asset to the teams that focus on those areas.
2. Have we overlooked any important areas? If so, why should we deal with them now? Are you the person in the class who can handle the job best?
3. Give a preliminary list of possible sources of information for the areas you are interested in. Explain why these areas are valuable sources.

This activity helps students to
1. work in areas in which they have some interest or expertise,
2. formulate persuasive arguments,
3. identify effective sources of information,
4. commit themselves to carrying out an assignment.

Individual presentations can be included so that each student can convince the group that he or she is the person to sit on a particular committee. Speaking to a friendly audience allows students to practice speaking skills, but also gives them practice in using listening, reading, and writing skills. A secret ballot based on the presentations that determines which students will serve on which committee will add more excitement to such a program.

Presenting oneself to a group is not an easy ask. Most high school students have never been—or have rarely been—the only person talking to a group, although they may have vast experience talking within a group. A checklist or worksheet can help these inexperienced orators prepare to speak effectively.

Exercise 4.3

Your speech will be more effective if you know what information you are going to present to the audience and if you assess what you know about the group you will be speaking to. The surer you are of why you should serve on a particular committee and the more convincingly you can present that reason to the class, the better are your chances of being elected to serve on the committee. As a beginning step in creating your campaign speech, answer the following questions. (In the blanks write the name of the committee on which you would like to serve.)

1. What skill or information do I have that is important to the _____ committee? (State the reason in one or two sentences.)
2. Why do I think the _____ committee is important? (One sentence.)
3. What one bit of information do I have now that will impress the class and show them that I am valuable for the reasons I have told them? (One sentence.)
4. What can I say to keep everyone's attention on me?
5. What must I not do or say to keep from boring, irritating, or making uncomfortable members of my audience?
6. In what order should I present my information?

This activity helps students to
1. assess and critique their knowledge of a particular body of information,
2. assess the biases and expectations of their audience,
3. create an effective appeal for their audience's support,
4. organize their speech.

CREATING WRITING/REPORTING AGENDAS

Writing is a craft that can be learned *only* through practice. As part of that practice, student writers need opportunities to have as many writing experiences as possible so that they can develop strategies to deal with them. Too often, however, high schools present pressure-laden writing situations to their students under the utilitarian, but inaccurate, assumption that these are the only writing situations students will experience in college or as members of the work force. Most people will write memos to their peers, directions about how to get to the company Christmas party, responses to class lectures, lab reports, letters, articles, job applications, loan applications, Sunday school lessons, grocery lists. Few of these writing tasks are perceived as being overtly formal or necessarily threatening. Yet, writing within specific time constraints is a skill students need to be familiar with because essay examinations *are* a major part of higher education and reports or letters *will* always be requested ASAP. Teachers, however, can devise many ways to introduce young writers to this type of writing.

Exercises 4.1, 4.2, and 4.3 ask students to respond to a series of queries within one class period. These activities require students to do much more critical thinking than does recalling what they did over the summer vacation, and they reduce the pressure that formal theme assignments sometimes generate. Students are asked simply to give important information to someone they know, thus having not only a purpose for both writing and speaking, but also a specific audience to write and speak to. Immature writers often lack purpose and a sense of audience. These are the problems most generic topics compound. When students know why they are writing and speaking and to whom, they write and speak more effectively.

Knowledge empowers the writer. Student writers need to know the *why,* and the *for whom,* behind their assignments because such information gives them the confidence they need to complete the task. Knowing *when* writing is due is also essential for writers because it allows them to plan and use the entire writing process rather than just the initial draft phase. But writing schedules need to have a reason behind their existence or they make the writing event meaningless, just a hoop for students to jump through. Incorporating all the dates into a larger agenda helps students understand the whole writing process as a unified activity.

When research and recommendation teams have been formed, the teacher can ask each group to create a timetable for its part of the class project. Students can plan their actions to fit their needs; they are wonders at finding the time to do all the last minute work before taking tests, or for planning their spring breaks to the minute. Too often, however, they are not encouraged to help plan their education, nor are they usually consulted about matters of scheduling. Yet, they *can* create agendas for completing products within general time frames, and when they do, students assume responsibility for some of the risks of their endeavors. They also get the job done.

Exercise 4.4

1. Give each team member a schedule of the grading period, indicating only the dates by which group projects are to be submitted. These projects can be one progress report (written and oral), one draft of the committee report in progress, and the final committee recommendations. Have all students examine their time commitments for the period under consideration, and create a calendar for their groups. Each committee member needs to schedule due dates for individual progress reports, for early draft sections of the committee's report, and for later drafts.
2. Ask all committees then to submit agendas they have created for themselves and they have agreed to.

This activity requires students to
1. set their own agendas, organize their time, and be responsible for a schedule;
2. work out a compromise on an agenda that reflects the needs of each particular group;
3. be responsible for meeting deadlines that affect the success of many people and groups.

Work that students submit for evaluation does not have to be earmarked specifically for the teacher's desk. The pressure of performing for one's peers is great, and can be used to ensure quality and timely submission of work if students are responsible to each other *as well* as to the instructor. A sobering thought is that teenagers typically are more concerned with the impression they make on their peers than on their teachers.

If authors submit drafts of their work to other members of the class for comments, suggestions, and editing, they can also receive a grade for doing the same for other classmates. More is at risk for students when their work is inspected by their friends, their enemies, or the objects of their affections than when teachers are their only critics.

Many options exist for developing writing programs in which students write and speak to their peers, their teachers, and possibly even their communities. Exercises 4.1, 4.2, 4.3, and 4.4 can be extended to allow students

- to write for readers other than their teachers,
- to use the whole writing process,
- to speak to a group of involved listeners,
- to rely on other writers for help and instruction,
- to contribute to a large project,
- to share responsibility for the project's immediate and overall success.

Exercises 4.1, 4.2 and 4.3 and 4.4 do not resemble most assignments in stereotypical English classrooms. Not once has there been a suggestion for a grammar lesson; not once has there been required reading of "great literature"; not once has there been a request for a formal theme. In fact, this model classroom resembles the real world, where people work with colleagues who share their interests. The multiple dialogues created by such learning environments are exactly what create an effective writing classroom. More significantly: *This mix is what turns any classroom into an effective learning classroom.*

At this point we expect many teachers to become either nervous about the classroom we are advocating, or to rise out of their chairs and demand that we address their concerns about doing the traditional jobs of English classes that have not been addressed specifically in our model. We agree. Now is a good time for us to deal with some of the recurring "But, what about . . . ?" questions.

BUT WHAT ABOUT LANGUAGE INSTRUCTION?

Children do not learn their first language by studying the grammar of that language formally. Instead they become fluent by using language to get things done—language proficiency springs from a desire to communicate. American educators, however, seem to forget or ignore this fundamental fact of language acquisition when they begin to lead students toward fluency in the language of most schools—standard English, whatever that is. English teachers seem to forget that while they may have been instructed about the structure of their language, the fluency they enjoy arrived by their using the language to communicate and to accomplish things they needed to accomplish. Yet, they are sometimes not willing to allow their students the same opportunities to discover and to learn how to manipulate English as a real, useful language. Too often English teachers treat their subject like a dead language, existing only as rules and structures. Then we wonder why students don't like English.

Students know the language; although they cannot always spot passive constructions or split infinitives or problems in agreement and reference, they know how to use the language effectively—that is, they know how to make themselves understood. They also are willing to pick up new information about the language *if* they can recognize a use for it. Writing they do for real purposes demonstrates to students the need for a better understanding of the weapons in their grammatical arsenals. Students know that writing they do for other people reflects directly on them as writers and as people—*if the writing is real*. They are willing to listen to instruction on particulars about mechanics of which they are uncertain; they are willing to learn options that exist for them within the language—if they realize a need for it.

The types of activities described in exercises 3.5 and 3.10 can be the base for not only expanding students' vocabularies in ways that allow them to communicate efficiently within several technical areas, but that also allow individual students to add to their peers' lexicons.

Exercise 4.5

1. On the chalkboard, write the following lists of words, or a similar list, each word of which one of the committees is likely to encounter or use in its research:

document	laser printer
password	byte
virus	megabyte
cursor	hardware
mouse	software
output	database
input	modem

   Make sure the words you select are used by an identifiable group of people—an industry, an academic discipline, a speech community. Ask students to arrange the list in alphabetical order, and then to create definitions for the words, noting their use as different parts of speech. Ask the class to discuss in what settings these words are normally used, and how these words are important to the class project.

2. Using the same list, have students find the following information about each word:

    a. its part of speech when used in the project's context,
    b. its etymology,
    c. a definition applicable to the class project.

3. Ask students to identify 20 words they have found to be used frequently in the field they have researched and that members of their committee and other students need to know in order to understand the findings of their research. Using the same instructions as in the previous activity, have students create a 20-item dictionary to accompany their research.

4. Have each committee compile a committee glossary, to append to their progress reports and to their final recommendations, that contains the five words from each member's dictionary that the committee thinks will give the class the most trouble.

These exercises help students to

1. expand their vocabularies,
2. work together to assess their peers' information needs,
3. locate specific types of information,
4. understand how words originate and change to fit communicative needs.

Students are not blind automatons. They know that grammar exercises are merely to be endured and that split infinitives are something to be filed away in short-term memory for Friday's quiz. The goal of language teachers, however, is to prove these assumptions false, to make their students' understanding of how our language works so crucially important that students want to master the information. Students are willing to be challenged and to learn, to engage in activities whose execution makes sense. The 30 teenagers arranged in five or six rows also know that orchestrating 16 or 18 weeks of grammar drills is not an activity that gives teachers the sense of accomplishment for which most of them went into teaching. Yet, some teachers appear to believe that, although it is not enjoyable, rote memorization of English grammar is the only avenue open to their students for attaining mastery of the language. Forced feeding of grammatical categories appears to some of them to be the pre-eminent instructional method.

64

Students will master the system. But that mastery comes most easily when students and teachers work one-on-one with each other and with other writers to meet their immediate needs rather than when teachers lecture on the use of the colon to classes in which three students want information about semicolons, two want to know the ins-and-outs of agreement, five have questions about rhetorical strategies, two are unsure about their use of commas, and one just wants to go to the restroom.

CONFERENCES: TEACHER-TO-STUDENT AND STUDENT-TO-STUDENT

What would your reaction be if you walked into a ceramics studio, were given a list of rules that define the medium and tell how it can be used, and were told to start throwing perfect pots immediately? You would definitely think that something was awry: Where is the potter to demonstrate how to use the potter's wheel, how to touch the clay, and how to understand the process by which raw clay is transformed into art? Yet most high school students are introduced to writing in a comparable way. They are given a handbook containing all the do's and don'ts that prescriptive grammarians have struggled to create for over 200 years and a list of composition modes considered valid. Then they are told to write. How often are they offered the chance to watch as their instructor demonstrates effective strategies for dealing with the complexities of writing? How often do apprentice writers get to show their premature efforts to an artisan in order to receive praise and the constructive benefit of that more practiced writer's experience? How often do students witness the fact that writing is a difficult endeavor for *all* writers as they watch their teacher struggle to write? In most classes, little time remains after grammar drills to do much beyond assigning the week's essay topic.

Writing is one of the few arts that has abandoned the traditionally close working relationship of teacher to student. Increasing numbers of writing teachers, however, strive to give developing writers the kinds of instruction and support that not only create learning that survives beyond next week's quiz, but that instills in these young writers a sense of purpose for their writing, a respect for the power contained in writing, and the confidence to know they can write successfully. Writing teachers like this talk to their students one-on-one about the work the students are engaged in. Not only do such teachers get to know their students as people with ideas to express and things to teach others, but these teachers also teach important skills.

The one-on-one writing conference is probably the most efficient instructional tool a writing teacher can employ.[5] Every teacher has experienced the frustration of seeing students' eyes glaze over while they are being talked at or lectured to. These teachers may have thought that if they could only deal with these students alone they could involve the uninvolved. That assumption is correct and provides the basis for one-on-one writing conferences.

Writing teachers who use the one-on-one writing conference understand that learning happens as the result of individual instruction. They also know that working with individual students—or even with a small group of students—allows the needs of these writers to be met as they surface rather than as skills listed on the syllabus that probably do not interest student writers. Writers who are shown how to circumvent a problem they face in a current piece of their own writing will employ that and other strategies in their future writing; they recognize a practical use for such knowledge and thus appropriate it.

A Few Suggestions for Conferences

1. Conference *during* the writing process.

Conferences are most effective when they are held *with* a piece of writing as the third member of the conference. These sessions are about writing, so the student writer needs to supply a manuscript to which the discussion can be directed. Conferences do not require completed texts—nor are such texts really desirable. Conferences are concerned with improving pieces *while* they are being produced; completed writing is completed writing—finished writing, an artifact, dead writing—and nothing is tougher to revive than a completed paper. Notes, outlines, early drafts, revised drafts, and false starts are the matters teachers discuss in productive conferences.

Exercise 4.6

1. Say to your students, "Have a member of your committee read the material you want to discuss before you come to your writing conference. Make notes so you can say quickly and smoothly what you need to say and do not end up wasting your partner's time. Provide your reader with the information asked for on this handout."

    a. What you think works well in the material, and why.
    b. What you think does not yet work as well as you would like.
    c. What important information you think might be missing.
    d. What you think you need to do next.

e. What grammatical or mechanical feature in the piece you are not sure you are using effectively.

2. After you have spoken with your classmate, ask for his or her comments about the piece of writing under review. Use these questions as starting points and take notes so that this advice is available when you work on the piece of writing again:
   a. What do you like the most in this piece? Why?
   b. What do you like the least in the piece? Why?
   c. Can you think of information I need to obtain to make the argument hold together? Where can I get it?
   d. Is there something else you think I need to know that I haven't thought of?
   e. How can you help me with my problems in usage and mechanics?

These activities help students to
1. take notes to ensure the success of a real communicative situation,
2. critique the effectiveness of their work-in-progress and also the work-in-progress of their committee members,
3. experience being responsible for teaching something to someone else,
4. look for missing pieces of an argument,
5. talk to their peers as excited, involved professionals.

---

2. Conference frequently.

The more opportunities apprentice writers have to show their work to their teachers for critiquing and to get answers to the problems facing them as writers, the better their writing will become. A class of up to 35 students can be dealt with as individual writers every other week without putting undue strain on the instructor. If we want students to believe that writing is important, they need to see their writing as important enough to merit frequent discussion.

3. Keep conferences short.

The only way to give all writers the attention they deserve is to keep conferences short so that every student can get the benefit of personal instruction. The most effective conferences have been found to last between five and ten minutes. This economy of time restricts both parties from straying off topic: What use is a writing conference that talks about the weather? Short meetings also encourage students to bring their most pressing problem to light, rather than talking about things they believe the teacher wants them to talk about. Seven students can be served within a 50-minute period if both teachers and students keep on task. At that rate, every student can be met once every other week, and time will still be left for other activities.

Conferences can be kept short and efficient if you ask your writers to supply you with the information requested in the following exercise.

Exercise 4.7

Have all students write a brief memo telling you
1. Where they are in their part of the project.
2. What they feel best about in the piece of writing they plan to bring to the conference.
3. What is bothering them about the piece at present.
4. One grammatical/mechanical issue they think they need to discuss with you.

This activity allows
1. students to help plan the conference agenda;
2. students to exhibit their critical reading abilities;
3. students to practice a form of communication common in both academia and business;
4. teachers to plan an efficient meeting with each writer;
5. the conference to be an individualized rather than a generic event.

---

4. **Listen. Don't Talk.**

Teachers talk too much. Conferences are designed to serve the needs of the student, but those needs cannot be identified unless the student reveals them. The one-on-one conference provides one of the few opportunities students have in formal educational settings to determine the agenda for a conversation. Not only do they need to gain experience in this activity as part of their vocational and social

68

training, but they need also to accept the responsibility for determining much of the effectiveness of the conference. An efficient conference participant listens to the needs of the other member.

5. Tutor. Don't Evaluate.

In the conference, students bring teachers their work in progress, work in the process of creation, work that is vulnerable. The role of the teacher at this point is that of a tutor, an artisan leading an apprentice, not that of an evaluator. Grades have no place in the conference; instead, the teacher teaches, guides, provides help, bolsters flagging confidences—all things good teachers do best. Give what help is needed, but do not solve students' problems for them. We learn best by solving our own problems, yet we are often aided by guides who lead us toward our solutions. Be a guide. Offer the use of your experiences. Offer the benefits of your expertise. The writing conference is the best situation in which to offer instruction in mechanics and usage as well, because it allows the teacher to show the logic behind rules when they are applied to real-language situations. Exercise 4.7, Item 4, for instance, allows language instruction to be introduced to the class as important to writing and meaningful to the writer.

6. Ask questions. Don't give answers.

Students are adept language users who can solve their own problems about its use. What they need from teachers usually is to be pointed in some direction, so that they don't waste inordinate amounts of time as they pursue their goals. The questions teachers ask serve that purpose: questions initiate conversations, questions set agendas, questions identify needs. From his many years of using the writing conference as his primary writing instruction tool, Donald Murray has found the questions that best open writing conferences are like the following:
   • What did you learn from this piece of writing?
   • What do you intend to do in the next draft?
   • What surprised you in the draft?
   • Where is the piece of writing taking you?
   • What do you like best in the piece of writing?
   • What questions do you have of me?[6]

BUT WHAT ABOUT DEVELOPING
CRITICAL THINKING SKILLS?

We traditionally require our students to write about and discuss literature in the English class as a means of developing their critical thinking skills. Such texts as Steinbeck's *The Pearl* or Hawthorne's *The Scarlet Letter* force students to deal with abstract concepts—duty, fidelity, justice, honor—and to invent a conceptual framework around which to structure their understanding of texts. Writing well about literature is demanding but rewarding for students. Many of them, however, are denied access to these experiences because the reading material is either alien to their social/ethnic community or does not connect with their immediate interests.

Many well-written books are available that appeal to those students who have little interest in "literature," and that can help these students build the critical thinking skills they need in order to succeed both in the educational system and in the workplace. For students from depressed economic backgrounds, much of the traditional canon, characterized by white middle-class literature, is meaningless. There are, however, biographies of men and women from situations like their own to read and to be challenged by. The novels of Toni Morrison, the essays and speeches of Martin Luther King, Jr., and even the movies of Spike Lee, can be used to provide these students with a way to read texts as an intellectual activity.

Those students interested in the sciences can also be challenged and encouraged to continue reading and thinking. Stephen Hawking's *A Brief History of Time* is a fascinating, well-written introduction to the principles that move our universe.[7] Hawking's writing is capable of intellectually challenging and adding to the expertise of the budding chemist, physicist, astronomer.

Teachers interested in fostering intellectual curiosity in all their students use whatever literature is available to them to meet the needs of each student. These teachers understand that exposure to texts is the means to a desired end—critical growth—rather than the end itself. Exercises 3.7, 3.8, and 3.9 work as well for demonstrating the development of critical thinking skills as for recording gains in reading abilities. Questions that can be added to those exercises that will force students to look behind the text and discover how its effects are achieved are the following:

1. How did your author keep your attention throughout the work? Did he or she rely just on a good story or did he or she manipulate the information in order to keep you reading? How was this done?

2. How did your author make you believe that the information in the book was accurate and that he or she was a credible source of information? Can you use this tactic in your own writing and speaking? How?
3. What would you have done differently in the work to make it more appealing to your friends?

The research conducted by the class committees requires students to read a variety of texts they do not usually encounter in traditional English classes. For example, books and articles that range from how-to manuals, to materials descriptions, to systems descriptions, to methods suggestions, to theoretical statements offer students an opportunity to interact not only with genuine writing—a work written to achieve actual ends—but to investigate the rhetorical principles that allow the text to be deemed successful—or in some cases, unsuccessful. These written materials can be examined and reported on using the type of inquiry suggested by Exercise 3.8, Item 2.

BUT WHAT ABOUT CRITICAL READING AND EDITING SKILLS?

The class project offers many opportunities, other than those we have previously discussed, to work on critical reading and editing skills. Committee members can serve as first readers for drafts of progress reports and committee findings. The more chances they have to work with other writers' writing in a setting where their own comments, editing, and suggestions matter and are considered valid, the better the chances are that students will recognize that these activities are important parts of the composing process, and will believe that they can effectively manipulate the language.

The first time students are told to work with someone else's writing, they are timid. They are afraid to trust their understanding of how the language operates and of what kinds of advice to give and how far to go in giving their help. Suggestions about how to approach a text as a critical reader and editor can help ease their initial reluctance.

Exercise 4.8

For early drafts:
1. Have students write for 10 minutes about what bothers them in their draft, and what they think are the piece's strengths and weaknesses.

2. Have students state one major concern about their drafts, other than their concern about their problems in usage and mechanics. Record these responses on the chalkboard and ask students to put a special mark beside concerns members of their committee have voiced.
3. Allow students to spend 30 to 50 minutes reading the draft of one of their committee members. Tell them not to be afraid to make any suggestions they think will strengthen the piece, and not to be hesitant about writing on the draft itself. Remind them to deal with the concerns stated by the author of the piece and the rest of their committee, and to be clear about what changes, additions, suggestions, or movements of material within the text they think will strengthen the writing.
4. Ask students to write a brief letter to the writer of the piece they read. The letter should include:
   • references to what they think works best in the piece, and why it is effective;
   • explanations of why they think particular changes need to be made; and
   • suggestions about what the author can do next.
5. Ask students to make copies of their drafts, so that you can also make suggestions about the research and its presentation. (At this stage you should resist the urge to mark mechanical or grammatical problems because to do so will communicate to students that you consider these surface matters to be of primary importance to you. If you call such matters to their attention, they will fix the problems and neglect the more demanding job of revising the draft.)

Exercise 4.9

For later drafts:
1. Have students submit one copy of their piece to a committee member and one to you. After both copies have been read and commented on, this time giving some attention to the surface features of the paper, allow the authors time to consult with their editors/readers about the suggestions that have been made. Such a discussion can be the topic of a writing conference.
2. Remind the students that their papers belong to them; therefore they do not have to accept any comments their editors make. They should incorporate only those suggested changes that

they think strengthen their text and that are in keeping with the goal they have for that piece of writing.
3. Have students write a memo to their peer reader/critic explaining which suggestions they have incorporated into their texts and which they have not. Encourage students to include the reasons behind their decisions.

These activities help students to
1. develop confidence in their abilities as effective critics of writing,
2. realize how their writing interacts with real readers,
3. understand the need to be clear and complete in their presentation of information,
4. develop their critical reading skills,
5. serve as tutors to other writers,
6. recognize the value of having outside editors.

BUT WHAT ABOUT EVALUATION?

At some point, all speaking and writing are completed—the speaker's time is up, the project is due, the mail carrier is at the mailbox, the class period is over. Writers release their grip on their creations at these moments and their writing becomes an artifact, a piece of public discourse, open to inspection and to critique. In high schools, this is the time at which most work is evaluated and grades are assigned. An inevitable part of the American education system, grades will not disappear regardless of the challenges leveled against their accuracy as indicators of students' development. What can change about grading is the philosophy teachers employ in the language class to guide evaluation and grade-giving.

Three-comma-splices-and-the-paper-fails is an arbitrary and unrealistic means by which to measure a writer's work. Too often, however, such standards have been used as yardsticks of writing acceptability in academic settings, regardless of their lack of correspondence to the world outside the schoolroom. This singular attention to the surface details of the text not only has earned English teachers reputations as grammatical bloodhounds, able to sniff out errors from 100 words away, but has also added to the misrepresentation that writing produced in school is done solely for the assessment of students' surface correctness.

A common fear among language arts teachers is that their grading of communicative efforts—oral and written—is arbitrary and idiosyncratic, that no one else grades quite as they do. *NO ONE ELSE DOES!* This grading insecurity has created the grammar bloodhounds who often communicate misleading messages to their students. All teachers can mark the same surface problems on a paper and thus appear to be grading consistently. What many teachers have failed to employ are the numerous options available that permit them to use more than their solitary voices in the evaluation process. They ignore the possibilities surrounding them for allowing work to be evaluated by the community: whether the academic community within a school's walls, a community of experts about the subject being communicated, or even a community of writers.

The progress reports, reports to committees, and final committee recommendations that are the products of the large projects discussed in this chapter can be evaluated by members of the academic community other than the teacher in whose class the work is accomplished. Two pools of evaluative assistants that can be drawn upon are the student authors themselves and other faculty members. Both groups of potential evaluators have an expertise that can be used to ease grading angst.

Students are writers-in-training. The development of their critical reading, critical editing, and communication skills can be viewed and enhanced by allowing them to play a part in the evaluation process of their own work. Letting students decide grades is not a realistic goal for most schools, but students can be used to create critical reading guides and evaluative glosses of their own work as a means of making teachers' evaluations more representative of an individual student's progress. The creator of a text knows more about that text's creation, structure, and development than any critic, so students can be involved in the evaluation process by writing critiques of the work they submit for evaluation. Writers' comments about their own work are valuable because they come from experts about each text, and teachers led through a student's work by the creator of that work are better able to witness the student's development as an effective communicator than when they venture into these texts with no knowledge of what they will find there.

Exercise 4.10

Today a paper is due for submission. Because you are the author of the piece to be evaluated, you know more about it and about your writing than anyone else. Please take the class period to complete the following assignment so that I can benefit from your expertise.

I will use your critique as a road map to your paper. It should allow me to find the points of interest along the way and to miss the tourist

traps. Please include the following information:
- What works well in the piece? Why? Give specific examples.
- What would you like to change? Why?
- Is there any place that bombs completely?
- Did the presentation form fit the information? How?
- Whom do you consider to be the paper's audience?
- How have you addressed that audience?
- How did you go about writing this piece?
- Has your approach changed since the last paper? Was it for the better?
- What will you do differently next time? Why?
- What one mechanical or structural problem would you like me to focus on when I read this paper? Why?

This critique may be more effective if you don't just answer each question individually. Most of the points in it work and interact with other points. A memo or a letter may be the most efficient way to get the information out. Or you may wish to use some other form of communication.

This exercise helps students to
1. participate to some extent in the evaluation process;
2. demonstrate their abilities to read their own texts critically, and to evaluate the effectiveness of their writing;
3. practice writing to a specific audience;
4. decide the best way to present information to a reader.

Principals and other faculty members can also serve as evaluators. Not only are they education experts, but they have experience producing the type of communication the students are producing and judging the effectiveness of the products. Bringing in evaluators from outside the classroom also gives students practice in writing and speaking to an audience other than their teacher, a chance they are rarely offered in school. Another group of outside evaluators is comprised of experts in the areas each committee researched. Local civic clubs are treasure troves of such expertise and are always on the lookout for services they can perform for the community. Using any—or all—of these sources of evaluators is good for the morale of the students, of the school, of the community because
1. students are allowed to experience communicating in realistic situations to an audience of interested experts and to experience hav-

ing these experts treat them as credible sources of information;

2. school faculties see engaged learning going on in their schools; such activity creates good feelings from administrations and more support and autonomy for teachers;

3. communities are involved in their children's education and that involvement usually creates good public relations for schools in an era when education is receiving considerable bad publicity.

The skills of encoding—speaking and writing—are hard to practice and develop apart from the skills of decoding—listening and reading. This inseparability is known to teachers who use whole-language approaches. Therefore, to maintain strict boundaries in the discussions or the exercises presented in this chapter would have been an unrealistic goal. Even though most of the material presented here focuses on speaking and writing, it also offers students many opportunities to listen and to read.

The writers hope that teachers who read this discussion on encoding will be able to use it to enhance their understandings of the complex activities required for students to be able to speak and to write effectively. We also hope that if teachers find our materials useful, they will tailor them to fit the unique situations and goals of their classrooms. A language arts program is most effective when the philosophy it advocates and the activities it employs meet the individual needs of its students.

Notes

1. See Donald Graves, *Writing: Teachers and Children at Work* (Portsmouth, N.H.: Heinemann Educational Books, 1983). See also Donald M. Murray, *Learning by Teaching* (Montclair, N.J.: Boynton/Cook, 1982), and Karen Spear, *Sharing Writing: Peer Response Groups in English Classes* (Portsmouth, N.H.: Heinemann, 1988).

2. See David Bartholomae, "Inventing the University," in *When a Writer Can't Write*, ed. Mike Rose (New York: Guilford Press, 1985). See also Karen Burke LeFevre, *Invention as a Social Act* (Carbondale, Ill.: Southern Illinois University Press, 1987), and James Moffett, *Teaching the Universe of Discourse* (Boston: Houghton Mifflin, 1968). Bartholomae's discussion of the social nature of writing is focused on writing within academic settings, while LeFevre and Moffett approach the topic from a more general and theoretical perspective.

3. The reports published by such researchers as Janet Emig, *The Composing Processes of Twelfth Graders* (Urbana, Ill.: National Council of Teachers of

English, 1971); Linda Flower and John R. Hayes, "A Cognitive Process Theory of Writing," *College Composition and Communication* 32 (December 1981): 365–87; and Sondra Perl, "Understanding Composing," *College Composition and Communication* 31 (December 1980): 363–69, demonstrated that writing is not a linear process, but rather a set of somewhat distinguishable activities that operate to allow writers to discover what it is they are trying to write, and develop that initial idea into a fully developed piece of writing.

4. See William E. Coles, Jr., *The Plural I: The Teaching of Writing* (New York: Holt, Rinehart and Winston, 1978). Coles was one of the first researchers to advocate collaborative writing assignments and group projects as an effective teaching tool.

5. See Muriel Harris, *Teaching One-to-One: The Writing Conference* (Urbana, Ill.: National Council of Teachers of English, 1986), and Donald Murray, *A Writer Teaches Writing* (Boston: Houghton Mifflin, 1985). See also Roger Garrison, "One-to-One: Tutorial Instruction in Freshman Composition," *New Directions for Community Colleges* 2 (Spring 1974): 55–84.

6. Donald M. Murray, *Learning by Teaching* (Montclair, N.J.: Boynton/Cook, 1982), p. 159.

7. Stephen Hawking, *A Brief History of Time* (New York: Bantam, 1988).

Chapter 5

COMMUNICATION SKILLS
AND A WHOLE-LANGUAGE APPROACH

Having read this far, you are surely aware that teachers committed to using a whole-language approach do not compartmentalize the various constituents of the communicative arts or of the English curriculum. This is because real-life situations constantly demand people to use all their communicative skills interactively. The whole-language approach also looks outside the physical confines of the school and does what it can to keep its students educationally involved with the broader community they are preparing to enter as workers and as voting citizens.

In ancient societies, children learned by following their elders and watching them work. They assisted them in some of the elements of their work, and as they grew to maturity, they took their places beside them as workers. In modern cultures with their decentralization, where jobs have become highly technical and where the workplace is not immediately outside one's door, it has been thought necessary and practical to separate students from the rest of society and to teach them in schools that serve as microcosms of the world they will eventually enter as full-fledged, contributing citizens. Such an arrangement is at best artificial, but practical considerations make it seem the best possibility for a society as large and complex as ours.

Ideally, the gap between schools and the real world should be reduced considerably. The whole-language approach can go far toward reducing this gap. The fact is that the world of work has changed much more rapidly than most schools have changed, widening the separation between schools and the world outside them. Home economics, vocational education, and distributive education programs have done much to reduce that separation, but teachers at all levels and in most subjects can do a great deal individually toward making schools more realistic microcosms—if they use their imaginations and if they draw on the community resources that are readily available to most of them.

This chapter proposes a coordinated method for achieving an effective educational dialogue between school and community, between students and adults, between groups with some common interest—a whole-language approach—by suggesting ways for teachers to bring volunteer consultants from the community into their classes. In order to help teachers capitalize on the potential for learning available within these dialogues, we suggest ways for students to participate fully in the interaction these meetings create by allowing students

1. to assume responsibility for planning,
2. to identify topics of interest and people to present them,
3. to invite and to receive the consultants,
4. to organize the activity, and
5. to write letters of thanks to those who have served as consultants.

If they use even some of the techniques that follow, employing only those they feel are appropriate to their individual situations and modifying them as they feel they must, most teachers will find that they are simultaneously bringing their schools and the community into closer harmony. They will also create situations in which their students necessarily use their communicative skills to accomplish practical and reasonable outcomes.

Working through parents and community service organizations, teachers can tap a wealth of resources that are theirs for the asking. The first step, however, is to get students to help teachers to identify both topics that relate to work they are doing in the English class and people who can help them work on various elements of those topics.

Exercise 5.1

1. Announce to your students that the class is going to draw up lists of topics that an outside consultant can be invited to present to and discuss with the class. Divide the class into groups of five or six students each. In 30 minutes or so each group should present a list of at least five topics members are interested in that have to do with some of the work they are doing or will be doing in class. The projects mentioned in Chapter 4 can be used as a base to help identify topics of interest. Groups should indicate possible activities for their volunteer consultants. Some of the following topics might be appropriate:
    - Tell about your job.
    - Tell how you use writing, reading, and speaking in your daily work routine.
    - Conduct a creative dramatic or improvisation session.

- Give a book review.
- Review a recent film, play, or rock concert.
- Tell how to write something for publication.
- Give a demonstration of how you create something.
- Show how to repair something, such as binding a book whose binding has been torn off.
- Tell how you get a newspaper ready for press.
- Show how you interview someone.
- Suggest ways to choose a college or technical school.
- Suggest ways to prepare for college or technical school.

2. Each group should list at least three possible learning outcomes for every topic it submits. These learning outcomes should have a direct relation to some area in the language arts.

This exercise helps students to
1. identify cogent topics for classroom discussion,
2. relate what they are learning in school to activities outside the school,
3. think in terms of what they can learn from an activity,
4. work together to achieve a stated, cooperative end.

Once students have settled on topics, have a committee review the suggestions from each committee to eliminate overlap. Because of overlap, the final list of topics in a class of 30 students will be somewhere between 15 and 20. Have a student or group of students reproduce all the topics so that every student can have a copy. Then have a member chosen by each group become part of a panel to discuss the topics and list them in order of the learning benefits that can accrue from each. This discussion should result in a list of no more than 10 topics that students will work from in the next exercise.

Exercise 5.2

Have students assemble in the same groups they were in for Exercise 5.1. Using the list of topics, each group's immediate task will be to decide what resource people are available to them either among their parents and other family members, through the school, or among other people they know in the community. Each group will submit a list of names with a brief description of how each person is uniquely qualified to talk or lead a discussion about something related to work students are doing or will be doing in their English class. Groups should identify specific learning outcomes. Make one or two telephone directories available to students so that they can give the address and telephone number of each nominee. This exercise should take about 30 minutes.

This exercise helps students to:
1. assess needs,
2. identify resources,
3. provide supporting materials,
4. identify possible learning outcomes,
5. work as members of a committee.

Exercise 5.3

A group of students should examine the list of possible consultants to eliminate overlap. They might also keep track of names that occur on several lists, because these will be the names of people the students would most like to hear from. A publishing group should assume responsibility for compiling the final list in a form that is easy to work with and for making the list available to every student in the class.

Once this list is available, the groups will reconvene. Each group will be assigned responsibility for two topics and will
1. decide approximately where in the semester calendar it would be most appropriate to have a consultant in for each topic;
2. decide which three people from the list of consultants would be best to consider for each topic;
3. rank those three nominees in order of preference, having two alternates in case the first choice cannot accept; and
4. reproduce this list, but not the rank ordering of the consultants—merely the topics, the dates, and possible consultants for each topic listed alphabetically.

This exercise helps students to
1. match people with topics by their ability and special training or interest,

2. realize the need for contingency plans should the first plan not work out,
3. organize events to coincide with what is going on in a course.

Once students have gotten this far, they need to decide how they will approach the person or people they plan to invite to participate in the activity they are arranging. Generally it is best to issue invitations in writing so that the consultants will have an opportunity to think over their responses. Therefore, having cleared the date, the topic, and the consultant with the teacher, each group should at this point compose a brief, direct letter to the consultant they wish to invite.

Exercise 5.4

Students will assemble in their groups. Their main task is to compose a letter of invitation and to decide whether the letters from all the groups should go out at once or whether they should go out three to four weeks before the date their topic is scheduled for presentation. Each letter should state the topic the students are interested in and the date they hope to have it presented. Students should make it clear that they can pay the consultant only with their gratitude, which, if he or she accepts, will be enormous. They should request a response by a given date, and they should clearly indicate to whom the responses should be directed by providing both an address and a telephone number for the person assigned to handle that detail. They should ask the consultants to provide brief background statements about themselves if they accept their invitations so their hosts can prepare introductions. Members of the group will be assigned other responsibilities, such as typing the letter and envelope, proofreading the letter, checking the dictionary for exact spellings, and doing polite followup if the person invited has not responded by the date stipulated. Once these letters are in final form, each member of the committee should sign the letter written by his or her committee, and the letter should be mailed. The group must also decide whether a followup letter of reminder or a telephone call close to the scheduled date of the presentation would be desirable.

This exercise helps students to
1. present details clearly in a letter,
2. decide what information *MUST* be included in a letter of this sort,
3. write letters using prescribed formats (invitations, business letters, thank-you notes, memos),
4. delegate responsibility.

As replies begin to come in, students will realize that sometimes they have to compromise on dates or that they have to adjust topics to suit the interests and abilities of the people they have invited. Each reply, whether it accepts or declines the invitation, must be answered politely. The group must compose letters that either express delight or indicate the hope that perhaps this person can come to the class at some future date. Letters to people who accept the invitation must include information about how to get to the school, about parking, about the amount of time available to the consultant, and about checking in first at the principal's office. A copy of this letter should be directed to the principal because it is to the main office that every visitor to a school reports initially.

Students now have to work on writing brief introductions for their speaker(s) based on the material the speakers have sent or on other material from such resources as *Who's Who in America, Contemporary Authors*, and similar reference works that are in most school libraries.

Exercise 5.5

1. Students should assemble in their groups. It is best if each member has a photocopy of the biographical material the proposed speaker has sent. Drawing on this material, each group member should write an introduction for the speaker of no more than 200 words. No more than 10 minutes should be spent on this activity. When visiting speakers are present, people want to hear them, not listen to long introductions. Nevertheless, courtesy decrees that some introduction be made. It should be brief, informative, and direct.
2. Each student should read aloud his or her introduction and should invite comments on it. After each introduction has been read, the group should decide who will introduce the visitor and which introduction will be used. Possibly the person who makes

the introduction will write a new one that incorporates elements from all the others.

3. At this point, too, the group has to arrange to welcome the visitor. Should the whole group go to the office for this purpose? Should anyone go to the office or should an office aide bring the speaker to the classroom? The group might also consider such questions as whether the speaker would like to use an overhead projector or a TV monitor or a VCR. These details should be worked out in advance.

This exercise helps students to
1. assume responsibility for arranging to have a speaker,
2. coordinate a complex activity so that everyone's best talents are used,
3. write with a clearly defined purpose in mind,
4. write with a clearly designated audience in mind,
5. consider matters of decorum.

If a consultant is coming to work with a class, members of the group responsible for arranging the event should be more knowledgeable than the rest of the class about the topic the speaker will address or the demonstration he/she will give. If the consultant is going to speak about international law, for example, students in the group that issues the invitation should know

1. what preparation one must have to become a lawyer,
2. what extra preparation it takes to specialize in international law,
3. what some of the major concerns of international law currently are,
4. how governments, all having different laws, interact legally.

This is just a partial list, A similar list could be drawn up for a guest who is to tell how being a garage mechanic requires reading, writing, listening, and speaking skills, or for a newspaper reporter who is to discuss interviewing techniques used in covering the news. If the visitor is going to conduct something that is process oriented, like leading a group in improvisation, members of the group that issued the invitation need to learn something about improvisation.

Exercise 5.6

1. Once the visitor has accepted the invitation, each member of the group should prepare a brief oral statement that gives some information about the topic the visitor will be focusing on. These oral presentations can be given to other members of the group, to the other committees, or to the class as a whole.
2. Each member of the inviting group should prepare one question to ask the visitor if there is a question-and-answer period, as there usually will be. Group members should screen these questions to assure that there is no overlap and that each question is pertinent to the topic.

This exercise helps students to
1. research a topic in a limited way,
2. discern what is pertinent to a topic,
3. organize information about a topic for oral presentation to a group,
4. listen critically to oral presentations,
5. coordinate their work to eliminate overlap.

Teachers who proceed with the program suggested here should be sure to receive administrative clearance. Most school principals are pleased to have interested members of the community come to the school to help enrich the curriculum and broaden learning. All principals, however, appreciate being informed of any activities out of the ordinary that are planned for their schools. As a matter of courtesy, teachers will keep them informed, preferably in writing, of a program that will bring outsiders to the school. As a matter of public relations, teachers can request that members of the school administration participate in the classes' activities as members of the audience or even as consultants. Invitations can also be extended to the staffs of school and local newspapers, of local television and radio stations.

Once consultants have been scheduled, teachers might wish to suggest to their classes how they can benefit most from the session that has been planned. The group that is directly responsible for each consultant's visit should be encouraged to make similar suggestions. Some consultants will make speeches that involve considerable specific information that should be taken down in students' notebooks. Others will involve students in activities or will offer demonstrations of techniques; the best response to each presentation will be achieved through planning in advance.

Teachers should also provide for follow-through the day after the consultant's visit. The inviting group might want to hold a panel discussion on the presentation and follow it up with some of the research they have done on their topic.

Exercise 5.7

The inviting group will have to work hard to prepare for the day after the presentation. Minimally, these students should have ready for distribution to all members of the class a summary sheet that addresses the previous day's activity. This summary sheet should create a focus for the panel discussion, which will be followed by questions and contributions from other class members.

The group will also have to convene within the next day or two to frame a thank-you letter to the consultant. It is important that this letter be written and mailed within two school days of the consultant's visit. The letter should not be pro forma. It should comment specifically on particular benefits the group feels its class derived from the consultant's presence. The letter need not be long, but it should be specific and sincere. It should also be signed by every member of the group.

This exercise helps students to
1. organize complex material,
2. meet a pressing deadline,
3. evaluate a public presentation,
4. direct a discussion,
5. write for specific reasons,
6. deal with matters of decorum.

Obviously, the major thrust of this chapter has been twofold. Reading it should encourage teachers to
1. give students responsibility for specific projects that involve people from outside the school, and
2. involve people from the community in the actual learning activities of the school.

This sort of approach can lead to other fruitful outcomes. For example, some of the consultants might be willing to have some interested students spend a day with them as they go about their work. Some might be willing to set up month-long internships for one or more graduating seniors during the last month of school, when "senioritis" afflicts many students who would work more productively outside the school than within it.

Through activities of this sort, teachers can sometimes initiate valuable public projects between service organizations and their students. Working with groups like the Lions Club, the Junior League, the NAACP, the Rotary, the Urban League, and other civic organizations, teachers might arrange for students and members of such organizations to

1. clean up a vacant tract of land that has become a neighborhood eyesore,
2. make regular visits to people in nursing homes,
3. make regular visits to children who have chronic illnesses and are in hospitals far from their homes,
4. arrange a letter exchange with foreign students who are studying English,
5. arrange a letter exchange with students from some other part of the country,
6. sponsor one or more foreign exchange students to study in the school district for a semester or a year,
7. beautify a strip of highway near or in their town,
8. grow vegetables to be contributed to a shelter for the homeless,
9. help some underprivileged people to paint or repair their homes,
10. go shopping once a week with an elderly person who needs help getting around and carrying groceries.

The more students are involved in the real world outside the school, the more likely they are to realize how the skills they use in school will serve them outside it. This realization will motivate them to pay attention to their school work. It may also encourage them to rebel against work they consider meaningless, but such rebellion is sometimes justified. If students are made to do something they can see no reason to do, and if the teacher cannot provide a convincing reason, then that activity needs to be reexamined and reconsidered. It is not the function of the American high school to turn out mindless automatons who obey without questioning.

The more the community outside the school is involved in the work going on inside the school, the more likely that community is to realize what the needs of its children are and how teachers are attempting to meet those needs. Knowing, rather than assuming to know, what schools are doing will motivate the members of the community to support those programs that involve their children in meaningful tasks, and to work to change those programs that serve no justifiable purpose. Parents who are informed about their children's education, and who have opportunitities to participate in those educational experiences are voters who will demand financial support for education, are citizens who will work with educators rather than against them, are watchdogs who will ensure that their community is being well served by its educational apparatus.

The whole-language approach will do a great deal to help teachers and students work together in harmony toward ends that have palpable practical outcomes. Through such activities, parents and other members of the community will be drawn into situations that help them to understand what the schools are trying to do and how they are trying to do it. This should make them a little less eager to criticize and more willing to understand the role public schools play in a free society.

ANNOTATED BIBLIOGRAPHY

Abrahamson, Richard F., and Betty Carter, eds. *Books for You: Booklist for Senior High Students*. Urbana, Ill.: National Council of Teachers of English, 1988.

This bulky volume provides the most comprehensive bibliography of books, most of them current, that are particularly appropriate for use in senior high schools. It is arranged topically and the annotations are clear and direct.

Applebee, Arthur. *Writing in the Secondary School*. Urbana, Ill.: National Council of Teachers of English, 1981.

This is the fullest report to date on what students actually write in all their classes in today's high schools. The book is especially instructive for teachers in all subject areas who want to teach writing skills that move beyond the five-paragraph expository or argumentative essay.

Bartholomae, David. "Inventing the University." In *When a Writer Can't Write: Studies in Writer's Block and other Composing Process Problems*, edited by Mike Rose. New York: Guilford Press, 1985.

This essay stresses the need for writers to become adept at communicating within the discourse of the academic community, because students' success often depends on that ability. If high school writing classes are to meet their students' needs, they must allow students to experience writing as experts. Thus students need to be allowed to write within areas they find interesting and meaningful.

Britton, James. *Language and Learning*. Hammondsworth, U.K.: Penguin Books, 1970.

Britton's book is central to understanding the significance of viewing writing as a process as well as a product. Britton's identification of the poetic, expressive, and transactional modes of writing and his assessment of how the expressive mode contributes and relates to transactional writing is thought-provoking.

_____, Tony Burgess, Nancy Martin, Alex McLeod, and Harold Rosen. *The Development of Writing Abilities (11–18)*. London: Macmillan, 1975.

This book provides some of the most convincing evidence of the need for students to write in all disciplines and to receive specific instruction in how to write in different disciplines.

Brufee, Kenneth A. "Collaborative Learning and the 'Conversation of Mankind.'" *College English* 46 (November 1984): 635–52.

Brufee explains how collaborative learning experiences not only give students a powerful tool by which to construct knowledge, but also help them develop the discourse skills needed to become participants in the academic community.

Calkins, Lucy M. *The Art of Teaching Writing*. Portsmouth, N.H.: Heinemann Educational Books, 1986.

Calkins discusses how to teach students to write poetry, fiction, and reports, suggesting valuable connections teachers can make between reading and writing. Her material about writing conferences is particularly useful.

Emig, Janet. *The Composing Processes of Twelfth Graders*. Urbana, Ill.: National Council of Teachers of English, 1971.

Emig examined closely the writing processes of a small number of high school seniors. She had them talk through their writing processes and identified two major kinds of writing: "reflexive," somewhat like Britton's expressive, and "extensive," somewhat like Britton's transactional. She urges teachers to pay greater attention to the reflexive than to the extensive, which will improve once the reflexive is properly employed.

Flower, Linda. *Problem-Solving Strategies for Writing*. New York: Harcourt Brace Jovanovich, 1981.

This textbook sets up writing protocols students can use to solve problems. It provides an excellent marriage between writing and logic. The book offers suggestions that are ideal for senior high school students.

Fulwiler, Toby, and Art Young, eds. *Language Connections: Writing and Reading Across the Curriculum*. Urbana, Ill.: National Council of Teachers of English, 1982.

This short book discusses the implementation of the writing-across-the-curriculum program that the editors helped to establish at Michigan Technological University, one of the first schools in the United States to introduce writing activities into every course in the curriculum. Much of the commentary carries over well into secondary schools.

Gilles, Carol, Mary Bixby, Paul Crowley, Shirley R. Crenshaw, Margaret Henrichs, Frances E. Reynolds, and Donelle Pyle. *Whole Language Strategies for Secondary Students*. New York: Richard C. Owen Publishers, 1988.

This book is eminently practical, providing all sorts of specific teaching techniques to supplement Dorothy J. Watson's theoretical chapter. A well-balanced presentation by people who work daily in schools and who understand students and their learning problems.

Golden, Catherine. "Composition: Writing and the Visual Arts," *Journal of Aesthetic Education* 20 (Fall, 1986): 59–68.

In this resourceful article, Golden shows how she used reproductions of three working sketches and the finished painting of Jean Auguste Dominique Ingres' *Portrait of the Comtesse d'Haussonville* to demonstrate to students that the process of revision pervades all creative endeavors from painting to writing sets of directions.

Goodman, Kenneth. *What's Whole in Whole Language?* Portsmouth, N.H.: Heinemann Educational Books, 1986.

This book is central to any thorough understanding of the whole-language theory of teaching. Its advice is practical and direct, its tactics realistic and easy to adapt to virtually any situation.

_____, E. Brooks Smith, Robert Meredith, and Yetta Goodman. *Language and Thinking in School—Whole-Language Curriculum*. New York: Richard C. Owen Publishers, 1987.

This book reviews salient research in learning theory and translates it into practical outcomes that teachers can use easily in a variety of teaching situations. The writers emphasize the relationship between the communicative skills and the development of effective thinking processes.

Graves, Donald H. *Writing: Teachers and Children at Work*. Portsmouth, N.H.: Heinemann Educational Books, 1983.

Graves's work has become a central text for whole-language teachers. He shows how students are willing to write when they are allowed some autonomy over their writing.

Harman, Susan, and Carole Edelsky. "The Risks of Whole Language Literacy: Alienation and Connection." *Language Arts* 66 (April 1989): 392–406.

This paper critiques whole language's theory in order to show that while whole language is the best classroom theory currently available, its practitioners need to be aware of the degree to which the assimilation of students into the classroom's social environment may be an act by which those same students can be excluded from their native cultures.

Harris, Muriel. *Teaching One-to-One: The Writing Conference*. Urbana, Ill.: National Council of Teachers of English, 1986.

This book should be required reading for any teacher employing whole-language methods in a writing class. Harris deals with not only the topography of writing conferences, but with their theoretical underpinnings as well.

LeFevre, Karen Burke. *Invention as a Social Act*. Carbondale, Ill.: Southern Illinois University Press, 1987.

While this book is theoretical in nature and uses a technical vocabulary, its comments on explorations of the social nature of writing make rewarding reading. LeFevre is especially useful when she deals with the power contained in collaborative learning and writing situations.

Manning, Gary, and Maryann Manning, eds. *Whole Language: Beliefs and Practices, K–8*. Washington, D.C.: National Education Association, 1989.

The contributors to this book have all had direct experience with teaching the whole-language approach at the grade levels under consideration. The suggestions are sensible and easily within the capacity of most teachers to implement.

Manning Gary, Maryann Manning, and Roberta Long. *Reading and Writing in the Middle Grades: A Whole-Language View*. Washington, D.C.: National Education Association, 1990.

This book is filled with suggested activities in reading and writing to use in whole-language classrooms. The ideas range from reading journals and choral reading to written conversations, letter writing, and ways to publish student writing. This is a realistically practical book for use by middle-level teachers and curriculum planners.

Manning, Maryann Murphy, Gary L. Manning, Roberta Long, and Bernice J. Wolfson. *Reading and Writing in the Primary Grades*. Washington, D.C.: National Education Association, 1987.

Although limited to the primary level, this book defines clearly what the whole-language approach is and demonstrates practical ways teachers can use this approach in the very earliest stages of formal education.

Moffett, James. *Teaching the Universe of Discourse*. New York: Houghton Mifflin, 1968.

Moffett shows how writers often move away from their audiences as they write and end up with lifeless, impersonally expressed products. He suggests ways to bring the thinking processes of students into line with their writing so that they will communicate in more authentic ways than many of them have generally been encouraged to do.

Murray, Donald M. *A Writer Teaches Writing*. 2d ed. Boston: Houghton Mifflin, 1985.

This book advocates teaching writing as a meaningful, important endeavor. Murray gives thorough advice about approaching all the facets of this task. His chapters dealing with conferencing are particularly important.

Nell, Victor. *Lost in a Book: The Psychology of Reading for Pleasure*. New Haven: Yale University Press, 1988.

This book will answer many questions teachers have about how to motivate students to read. The approach is sound, intelligent, and intellectual in the best sense. The author makes the information in the book easily accessible by his clear exposition and sensible structure.

Newman, Judith M., ed. *Whole Language—Theory in Use*. Portsmouth, N.H.: Heinemann Educational Books, 1985.

Perhaps the most valuable portion of this book has to do with how whole-language teachers conduct frequent conferences with their students so that they can direct their work realistically and effectively. It touches also on such practical matters as spelling, reading imaginative literature, and building a classroom atmosphere that encourages language learning.

Odell, Lee, and Dixie Goswami, eds. *Writing in Nonacademic Settings*. New York: Guilford Press, 1985.

The 14 essays in this collection offer the best overview in print of the actual writing tasks that people are called upon to perform in their workplaces.

Polanyi, Michael. *Personal Knowledge: Towards a Post-Critical Philosophy*. Chicago: University of Chicago Press, 1962.

This seminal book spawned much of the research done in composition theory from the late 1970s to the present. Polanyi's theory of tacit knowledge is the linchpin of much future thinking and writing about the relationship between writing and knowing.

Shaughnessy, Mina P. *Errors and Expectations: A Guide for the Teacher of Basic Writing*. New York: Oxford University Press, 1977.

Shaughnessy gives details about her attempts to bring functional literacy to inner-city students in the New York university in which she taught when functional illiterates were admitted under the "open-door" policy. Her brilliant diagnoses of the writing (and thinking) problems of these severely handicapped students have broad, general applications.

Smith, Frank. *Insult to Intelligence: The Bureaucratic Invasion of Our Classrooms*. New York: Arbor House, 1986.

Smith's critique of the way that everyone except teachers can control the education of our children is particularly cogent to the whole-language philosophical stance. This book is frank, compelling, and, above all, well written. The chapter dealing with good teaching champions whole language and demonstrates how it can reduce the detrimental impact of non-educators' demands on the educational system.

Turbill, Jan. *Now We Want to Write*. Rozelle, N.S.W., Australia: Primary Education Teaching Association, 1983.

This short book presents a rationale and suggestions for implementing a whole-language communication program in schools.

Vygotsky, Lev Semenovich. *Thought and Language*. Eugenia Hanfmann and Gertrude Vakar, trans. Cambridge, Mass.: Massachusetts Institute of Technology Press, 1962.

Vygotsky establishes a crucial relationship between speaking and thinking; from this grows the concept of "inner speech" that is fundamental to James Britton's conception of the expressive mode in writing.

Zinsser, William. *On Writing Well*. New York: Harper and Row, 1988.

Zinsser, who makes his living by writing, offers some of the most palatable and practical advice available to writers today. His book is a model of excellent writing; his suggestions are practical and reasonable. If you never read another book about writing, read this one!

_____. *Writing to Learn*. New York: Harper and Row, 1988.

Positing that writing is the logical arrangement of thought, Zinsser goes on to demonstrate how people learn by writing, how they order what they already know, often arriving at new and more complex understandings as the writing process proceeds. The book is highly readable and leads readers to valuable, sometimes profound, insights.

INDEX